COMMUN
WITH IM

Key Career Skills

by

S D Probert and J R Jammes

Atenar

Published by
Atenar Publishing Ltd
St Frideswides Cottage, Osney, Oxford, UK

First Edition 1996

British Library Cataloguing in Publication Data.

Probert, S.D.
Communicating with impact : key career skills
1. Interpersonal communication   2. Oral
communication   3. Written communication
4. English language - Usage
I. Title   II. Jammes, J.
302.2

ISBN: 0 9527744 0 2

Printed and bound in Great Britain by
Biddles Ltd, Guildford and King's Lynn

Contents

PREFACE - THE PROBLEM

Books on the proper use of the English language abound. Too often however, they are boring recitals of what should **not** be done. Admittedly, there is need for such guidance to be given to even the principal bodies in England, e.g. as is exemplified by the following recent quotation, concerning a 'Housing and Building Control Bill' from Hansard - i.e. the record of the proceedings of the Houses of Parliament, London:-

"Returned from the Commons with one of the Lords amendments to a Commons amendment disagreed to but amendments proposed in lieu thereof; with the Commons disagreement to the Lords amendment on which the Lords have insisted and the Commons amendments in lieu thereof not insisted on but with an amendment to the said Lords amendment and with consequential amendments to the Bill; with Commons amendments to a Lords amendment to which the Lords have disagreed not insisted on; with certain Commons amendments to another Lords amendment to which the Lords have disagreed not insisted on but amendments proposed in lieu thereof; and with the remaining Commons amendment to the Lords amendment to which the Lords have disagreed insisted on with a reason for such insistence." This is probably exact, but what does it mean?

The present slim volume attempts to be more positive and offers the authors' unequivocal opinions and simple recommendations with respect to achieving less ambiguous presentations. It offers hints for becoming more effective at achieving successful communications. This basic tool kit for life has no scholastic pretensions. We hope, for the reader, that the covers of this book, when shut, are not too far apart.

Most of us are often poor communicators. We need to practise to develop the skills to ensure that (i) unambiguous messages are conveyed to the right person at the right time and (ii) the messages received are correctly understood. But many devote little effort to managing properly the use of language. We rarely acknowledge that brief, clear, accurate and relevant instructions, reports and conversations, in plain English, can lead to a more effective use of time, less duplication, improved industrial relations and so higher probabilities of success.

Basic advice concerning how to make presentations, in formal situations, is presented in this volume. Much more than the exact use of words is required. Wise planning, preparation, organisation and practice will lead to far less effort being wasted. Increasingly, in order to possess a competitive edge, one needs (i) a high degree of inter-personal skills (e.g. to motivate others), and (ii) to be impressive in presenting oneself persuasively **in person**, as well as on paper.

Although human beings possess naturally a language instinct, the literacy levels of many young people, **with degrees or other commensurate professional qualifications**, in Britain, entering industry and commerce "are a national disgrace" (Lamb 1994). These youths tend too often to be incompetent at writing reports, drafting memoranda, producing single-page well-focused agenda, collating the minutes of meetings, applying for jobs, as well as at giving oral presentations. A recent survey, conducted by Bernard Lamb, of almost 250 British firms revealed that 16% of their young employees, with further or higher educational qualifications, are poor with respect to the use of written English, 40% adequate and 43% good. Ten percent are also considered to be weak at spoken English. While these figures are significantly better than for the whole 16 to 18 year-old group of youths in the general population, they are disappointing for such highly-trained, high-ability people (Wells, 1994). However, this is not surprising because the trend, during the last 30 years, is that graduates have become more numerate, but simultaneously less capable of effective verbal communications. Thus, now, more than one-third of employers in the UK spend money trying to raise the literacy levels of new recruits. Among the many pertinent pleas from UK industry and commerce are the desires to recruit personnel who are capable of (i) using the English language effectively; (ii) writing straight-forward messages; (iii) collating information logically; (iv) committing, in essence, ideas, thoughts and conversations accurately to paper; (v) avoiding the adoption of strong opinions from the poorly informed; and (vi) bidding successfully for financial support.

To improve your command of the English Language, you are recommended to consult regularly Sir Ernest Gowers' "The Complete

Plain Words", Pelican Books, 1971 and H.W. Fowler's "Dictionary of Modern English Usage", Oxford University Press, 1983 to supplement the advice given in the present text.

The rewards of a more exact use of the English language are manifold. Unambiguous speech and writing lead to more easily comprehensible instructions and engineering manuals, and so to fewer hazards and life-threatening situations. Although we pay lip service to this assertion, too often it is not implemented. As a result, we waste time and effort!

Part of the reason for this toleration of high levels of inexactness and ambiguity is the knock-on effect of the careless domestic use of the English language, and sometimes our lack of awareness of what standards should be expected. Also, inarticulateness increases unless we practise regularly communicating accurately and persuasively, and avoid being dominated by one-way communications (e.g. from TV and the more popular newspapers). 'Less box and more good books' is a wise slogan. While numeracy of the general population is improving, literacy would appear to be declining!

We would recommend the following: -

* Comprehensive, accurate, relevant instructions and reports, in plain English, can lead to a more effective use of time, reduced duplication of effort, fewer accidents and deaths, less overall energy expenditure and an increased probability of success.

* We can ill afford a lax attitude to the use of language, which is basic to our civilisation: it is our duty to make each word 'pull its weight', i.e. be brief and effective.

* We need to fine-tune our communication skills if we are to:
  (i) work together successfully in teams;
  (ii) develop an appetite for further education.
By becoming a more life-long learning society, the UK's competitive edge with respect to world trade, should be improved.

* In several aspects of the UK's education service, we need to 'move forward to basics', and in particular to give the exact use of the English language, once more, the educational attention it deserves!

1 THE ENGLISH LANGUAGE

Evolution

There are more than 5 million different words in the English language: the Oxford English dictionary (1994) contains the meanings of 616,500 words; William Shakespeare used about 15 thousand, Milton about 8 thousand and the Old Testament contains 5,642 different words. The average indigenous Briton employs about 4300 different words, but understands the exact meaning of only approximately 70% of these. Too rarely does the average Brit consult an English dictionary; often guessing the meaning of an unknown word from the context in which it appears. Thereby s(he) builds up and perpetuates a vocabulary of misunderstood words. Thus it is wise to consult a dictionary (and/or a thesaurus for synonyms and antonyms) immediately you encounter a spelling or an exact meaning problem. There are now cheap pocket computers available, each with more than 80 000 words in their memory and which can help in this endeavour.

English is a rich, living and rapidly-evolving language, so it is unwise to be pedantic and disparage all recent trends. Let us think back one generation in England, e.g. prior to AD 1939, then the following artefacts or concepts rarely, if at all, existed:- ball-point pens; computer dating; contact lenses; credit cards; day-care centres; electric blankets; FM-radio; instant coffee; penicillin; the pill; tumble driers; sheltered accommodation; software; videos and word processors. The term "making out" then referred to how well you did in the recent examination; "stud" was a device for fastening a collar to a shirt; "going all the way" meant staying on the bus to the terminus; a "gay" person was the life and soul of the party and nothing more; "coke" resided in the coal house; "grass" was mown, not smoked; "pot" was something you cooked in; and a "joint" referred to the meat you ate on a Sunday. Changes in our language are occurring more rapidly than even before.

On a more amusing note about the meaning of a word: several years ago, at a meeting with a student who had committed a minor misdemeanour, one of the authors told him 'I have to admonish you concerning ...'. His immediate reply was 'Thank you very much: I thought I was going to be told off'.

Sometimes words, even scientific ones, can have radically different meanings according to their contexts, e.g. lumen, which can mean either a unit of luminous flux, or a cavity within a plant cell, or a passage in a tubular organ.

With more than 9 hundred million people already speaking English **worldwide** - it is the international language of business - there are inevitably many forms of the language, and they are evolving rapidly, partly because of the global entertainment industry based on American English. English is now the world's lingua franca because of its inherent flexibility. Our European neighbours and partners display a prodigious keenness to learn it: e.g. 80% of all French, Italian and German secondary-school pupils study English. In the Netherlands, this proportion reaches 90% and in Denmark 96% of the whole population can converse effectively in English.

English is the obligatory international language for air-traffic control in order to try to ensure world-wide comprehension, but when "heavy" foreign accents or different concepts of grammar have crept into the radio transmissions, lives have sometimes been lost. Computers possess their own exacting standards of literacy, as is soon apparent when a comma is inserted in the wrong place in a computer program. However, confusingly in cyberspeak on the Internet, a "window" is something you open or close but never look through, whereas a "desktop" has a **vertical** screen. Also the wide difference between the Queen's English and American English can be misleading: for instance, in the UK we would say 'car boot' and 'condom', whereas in the USA the equivalents would be 'trunk' and 'rubber' respectively. (Further examples are given in Appendix 1.1).

Mis-use of words

Technical and business communications are often confusing because of the **buzz phrases** that are used in ways far removed from the contexts for which they have well-defined meanings. Examples like 'integrated climatic impact', 'parallel managerial concept' or 'balanced simulated algorithm': sound impressive and are only rarely challenged as to their exact meaning. However, they contribute considerably to vagueness and so should be pruned ruthlessly from your communications.

Endeavour to use familiar, non-technical words in general communications. Even for technical writing, it is wise to use plain (rather than flowery), non-esoteric language. Jargon and acronyms should only be employed when addressing those in the same discipline, and even then only accurately and sparingly. Unfortunately, jargon from one profession creeps contagiously into others, and is used in ways which differ from their originally well-defined meanings. It may sound impressive, but can lead to ambiguity.

In addition, redundant words, such as those shown in italics in the folowing phrases *'old* veteran' 'red *in colour'* and 'round *in shape'* should be edited out. See also Appendix 1.2.

Sir Winston Churchill's advice (in London, November 2nd 1949) was *"Short words are best and old words, when short, are best of all"*. The use of short, common words, provided they describe accurately what you want to say, is likely to lead to your statements having greater impact as well as being better understood.

The excessive repetition of a word in a conversation or a written report can be irritating and boring.   Use a thesaurus (e.g. The Collins English Dictionary and Thesaurus, Harper Collins, London 1993) to find alternative and sometimes more appropriate words.

Tautology, redundancy and circumlocutions are rife in modern English - see Appendix 1.2 - but should be avoided since they obscure swift and accurate understanding. The words in the left-hand column of Appendix 1.2 should be employed sparingly with a bias towards using instead the recommended alternative in the right-hand column.

Slovenly Use or Interpretation of the English Language.
Unfortunately, this occurs too frequently, but of greater concern is that we may not recognise these mistakes when they are made. However, we cannot afford such self-deception (i.e. that all is well with our

communication skills). Let us try to shock you into accepting that improvements may be needed! Consider the following examples: -

- 'We had *friends for tea*' - overheard at a bus stop. This does not imply a resurgence of cannibalism.

- 'The manager has personally passed all the water served here' - sign in a hotel in Mexico.

- 'Guaranteed no chemicals used' - on a restaurant menu in Canada.

- 'Carpet salesman required for covering the *whole of Yorkshire*' - advertisement in the trade press.

- Frequently heard in conversation: *'That's funny*', when something unusual happens, even when the occurrence may not be in the least amusing to the speaker.

- Have you ever *borrowed a match*? Was it really your intention to return it after use?

- 'Ears pierced *while you wait*' - notice in a shop window.

- *'Crash course for drivers*' - advertisement in a local newspaper. It is hoped that the instructions provided will lead to the avoidance of crashes, i.e. exactly the opposite meaning to that stated.

- Have you ever been asked, very politely, in a public library *'Is anyone sitting there*?, when there obviously is a *vacant* seat next to you.

- *'Charles has a temperature*' - BBC news. This implies Charles is ill: but we all have temperatures.

- *'Fly-tipping*' means the deliberate dumping of rubbish in an unauthorized place rather than the *"tipping of flies"*.

- Have you ever *'boiled a kettle, an egg or potatoes'*? Surely it is the water that boils!

- An *'Air Transport Company'* does not have the transport of air as its main aim, otherwise it would soon go out of business.

The intended meanings of these trivial examples are usually well understood, and so their inexactness is too easily excused. However, such ambiguities also occur in important, more complicated, less easily comprehended correspondence and can even lead to life-threatening situations!

The use of the hyphen or connecting link

This is recommended:-

* in commonly-employed expressions such as co-operation, co-ordination, de-ice, door-to-door, ex-teacher, fact-finding, five-year-plan, French-speaking, get-together, middle-aged, mother-in-law, open-air, passer-by, phone-in, shell-like, thirty-one, Vice-Chancellor, weather-beaten and X-ray.

* to help avoid ambiguity in expressions, viz.,

a French-history teacher	a French history-teacher
a heavy-oil engine	a heavy oil-engine
a little-used car	a little used-car.

APPENDIX 1.1 - American English

For the sake of avoiding misunderstandings, the following counterparts may be found helpful:

UK	USA
bank holiday	legal holiday
barrister, solicitor	attorney
bonnet (car)	hood
call box	phone booth
chips	french fries
crisps	potato chips
courgette	zucchini
cupboard	closet
drawing pin	thumbtack
draughts (i.e. a game)	checkers
first floor	second floor
flat (house)	apartment
fortnight	two weeks
gents (toilet)	men's room
ground floor	first floor
interval	intermission
jug	pitcher
lavatory	washroom, restroom
lorry	truck
motorway	freeway
nappy	diaper
nought	zero
petrol	gas
postcode	zip code
queue	line
roundabout	traffic circle
saloon car	sedan
swede (vegetable)	rutabaga
tap	faucet/spigot
toll (motorway)	turnpike
wing (car)	fender
zip fastener	zipper

APPENDIX 1.2 - Circumlocutions and tautology

AVOID	APPOSITE REPLACEMENT
a downward plunge	plunge
absolute certainty	certainty
added bonus	bonus
added extra	extra
advanced warning	warning
afford an opportunity to	allow for
an audible noise	noise
an oral presentation	a talk
an essential prerequisite	prerequisite
are of the same opinion	agree
at some future time	later
at that point in time	then
at the present (this moment in) time	now
bang up-to-date	up-to-date
by means of	by
circle round	circle
completely surrounded	surrounded
consensus of opinion	consensus
consequent upon	because of
considerable amount of	much, many
during such time as	while
during the period (time) that	while
fewer in number	fewer
for the reason that	because
forward planning	planning
free gifts	gifts
general consensus	consensus
I beg to differ	I disagree
I myself would disclaim	I disclaim
in conjunction with	with
in spite of the fact that	although
in the event that	if
in the vicinity of	near
in this day and age	now
in view of the fact that	because

Circumlocutions and tautology - continued....

AVOID	APPOSITE REPLACEMENT
in view of the foregoing circumstances	therefore
it is apparent therefore that	therefore
it may be said that	possibly
it may, however, be noted that	nevertheless
it was observed that	we observed that
management are	management is
meeting (up) with	meeting
necessitate	need
not infrequently	often
nothing if not	very
of a reversible nature	reversible
on a regular basis	regularly
on account of the fact that	as
on the grounds that	because
(owing to) the fact that	because
past history	history
regardless of the fact that	although
revert back	revert
serves the function of being	is
shortfall in supplies	shortage
square in shape	square
subsequent to	after
there can be little doubt that	this is probably
they are in fact	they are
to meet together	to meet
unjustly persecuted	persecuted
until such time as	until, till
utilise	use
where are you domiciled?	where do you live?
(which) goes under the name of	(is) called
with regard to/with respect to	about, concerning
with the exception of	except

2 HIGH - IMPACT COMMUNICATIONS

Aim for excellence, but don't expect perfection.

Assertions

In the increasingly high-technology affluent parts of our society, there are growing demands upon the available time of those in employment. So we need to be better organised in order to be more effective. One of the main management tools for reducing energy wastages (and the associated human mental-effort required) is via prior comprehensive planning and effective organisation of the ways in which the required proposed tasks are to be undertaken.

The flow-chart approach

An effective way of ensuring that a plan is implemented successfully is to be guided by a simulation **flow-chart** (see e.g.Figs. 2.1 and 2.2), designed by experts in the considered field, concerning the sequence of the main desirable activities and the associated decisions that need to be taken. This expert-system approach, when carried out in detail, eliminates the possibility of forgetting something essential at the "right" time, because the prescribed procedure will incorporate all the best relevant-practice steps not incurring excessive cost. However, it should be remembered that it is the high quality of the end-product which is important, rather than merely taking the "right" actions as a routine guided by the flow-chart.

The achievement of rigorous, persuasive analyses and/or syntheses usually requires:- (i) the adoption of only wise assumptions; (ii) remaining logical throughout; (iii) avoiding the introduction of ambiguities and unnecessary repetitions; (iv) the accurate use of appropriate language; as well as (v) being sufficiently comprehensive yet succinct. The resulting statements should lead eventually to fewer misapprehensions, mistakes and accidents, and hence to less energy expenditures, occurring. Obtaining such clear presentations, can be helped, at least partially, by systematically devising and employing flow-charts of the essential activities. For example, research reports would be more rapidly understood (and so less intellectual effort would be wasted by the reader), if, following the "Abstract", a well-designed flow-chart for the text were presented in the report. A flow-chart given at the outset of each chapter of a book would help students when revising the contents of that chapter. The presence of good flow-charts could also eliminate, in some instances, even the necessity for a "Contents" page in a report or book.

Example

The very abbreviated, outline flow-chart shown in Fig. 2.2, is offered as a check-list reminder of the activities in the commonly-occurring situation of **job hunting** - see also chapter 4. It is neither unique nor necessarily the best procedure for a particular requirement, but it does provide a first-approximation to best practice. Other charts should be developed so that you build up a personal portfolio of such guides for your main communication roles. It is often sensible to plagiarize from one chart when devising another (so that the good habits developed for one role reinforce those for another). For instance, the activities involved in preparing and giving an after-dinner speech are in many ways similar to those for presenting a formal lecture, except that, for the former, the humorous and anecdotal percentage of contents is usually greater, and the duration (~20 minutes) considerably shorter. The after-dinner speech is intended more to entertain rather than to inform; the speaker usually appearing to talk entirely "off the cuff" or employing only brief notes to remind him/her of the key points. An **after-dinner speech** should be like a lady's dress: long enough to cover the subject but short enough to be interesting!

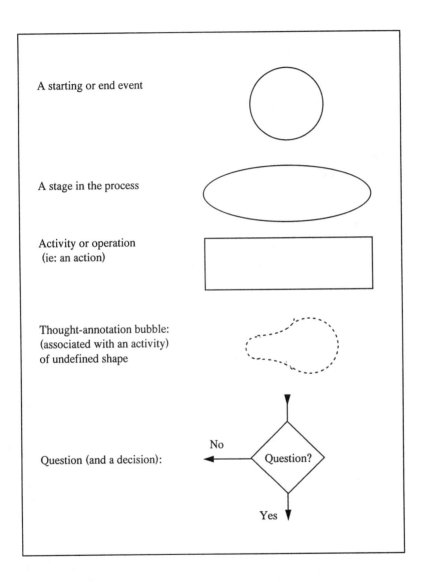

Figure 2.1. Conventionally-employed symbols for flow-charts

Figure 2.2 Flow-chart for job seeking.

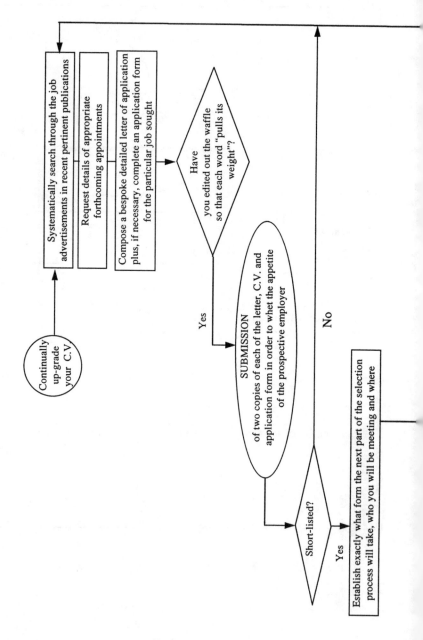

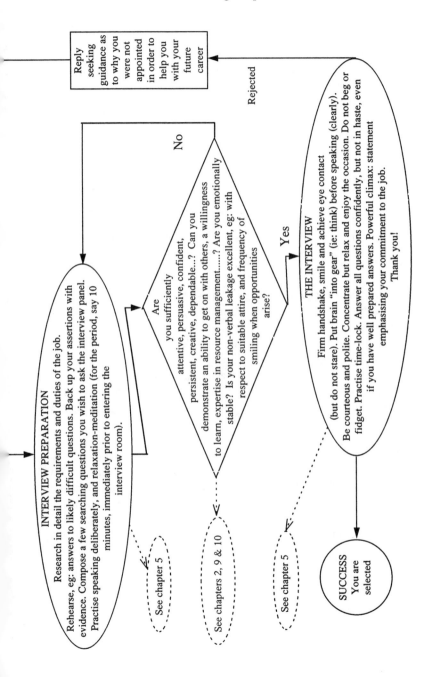

INTERVIEW PREPARATION
Research in detail the requirements and duties of the job. Rehearse, eg: answers to likely difficult questions. Back up your assertions with evidence. Compose a few searching questions you wish to ask the interview panel. Practise speaking deliberately, and relaxation-meditation (for the period, say 10 minutes, immediately prior to entering the interview room).

See chapter 5

Are you sufficiently attentive, persuasive, confident, persistent, creative, dependable..? Can you demonstrate an ability to get on with others, a willingness to learn, expertise in resource management....? Are you emotionally stable? Is your non-verbal leakage excellent, eg: with respect to suitable attire, and frequency of smiling when opportunities arise?

See chapters 2, 9 & 10

No

Yes

Reply seeking guidance as to why you were not appointed in order to help you with your future career

Rejected

THE INTERVIEW
Firm handshake, smile and achieve eye contact (but do not stare). Put brain "into gear" (ie: think) before speaking (clearly). Be courteous and polite. Concentrate but relax and enjoy the occasion. Do not beg or fidget. Practise time-lock. Answer all questions confidently, but not in haste, even if you have well prepared answers. Powerful climax: statement emphasising your commitment to the job. Thank you!

See chapter 5

SUCCESS You are selected

The importance of exact communications

A systematic task-oriented approach to life can, *very approximately*, be described by the following word equation: -

$$\left(\begin{array}{c} \text{Overall value achieved} \\ \text{by completing the project} \end{array} \right) =$$

$$\left(\begin{array}{c} \text{Worth -} \\ \text{whileness} \\ \text{of the} \\ \text{aim(s)} \end{array} \right) \times \left(\begin{array}{c} \text{Quality \& effectiveness} \\ \text{of the means devoted to} \\ \text{undertaking the project \&} \\ \text{arriving at the conclusions} \end{array} \right) \times \left(\begin{array}{c} \text{Effectiveness} \\ \text{of commun -} \\ \text{icating the} \\ \text{conclusions} \end{array} \right) \times \left(\begin{array}{c} \text{Degree of} \\ \text{success in} \\ \text{implementing} \\ \text{conclusions} \end{array} \right)$$

The relentless pursuit of **perfection** and total success leads to disappointment and misery because such goals are inevitably unobtainable, i.e. it is preferable to strive for excellence rather than for perfection. Be a 70% person: trying to achieve the remaining 30% is rarely worth the expenditure of the extra effort required. Therefore, it is wise to choose worthwhile, **realistic**, achievable goals. As you become more successful, make your goals more challenging. In this way, you grow to believe in yourself - i.e. you develop your self-esteem and a positive attitude.

If any one of the factors on the right-hand side of the equation tends to zero, then the value of the whole project is destroyed. For example, if the aims are not worthy of the expenditure of the effort, why bother with the project! Also, from the equation, it can be readily appreciated that skills in oral and written communications need to be highly developed if justifiable aims in any project are to be achieved.

18

3 COMMUNICATING ON FORMAL OCCASIONS

"If men would only say what they have to say in plain terms, how much more eloquent they would be"! - *On Style, Samuel Taylor Coleridge (1772-1834)*

Check List

Communication is the transfer of information and understanding from one person to another or to a group. Irrespective of what occasion, the basic essentials in the preparation for effective communication are:

- **clarify** your aims, objectives and issues;

- **focus** on your target audience or reader, by only offering what is wanted by them: avoid unnecessary details;

- **select** appropriate up-to-date material: irrelevant information obscures the message you wish to transmit;

- use only **clear, unambiguous statements** - avoid jargon, it can easily confuse and embarrass those unfamiliar with it;

- arrange your material in a **logical order**;

- **summarize**, in easily-understood language, the main conclusions; and

- **check** that your proposed timing is wise and acceptable: for instance, you will only capture your audience's full attention if the information is presented at a **suitable time** (e.g. not after a heavy meal).

Your role will be to (i) interest, motivate and challenge, (ii) pitch your presentation at not too high or low a level for your readership or audience, and (iii) show enthusiasm for the topic being presented.

Oral Communications

Remember "Stand upright to be seen, and speak up to be heard".

Non-verbal leakage

To be effective involves much more than employing the right words in the right sequence in the right context. For instance, do you appear to be relaxed and to act with confidence when in unfamiliar, challenging situations? Or are you ill at ease? Are you cool, calm and collected when speaking to an audience? Do you convey an aura of being a winner, i.e. of being successful, or do you lack a confident presence? Do you smile sufficiently often? Have you an acceptable image? In effect, do you "look the part"?

Let us consider some of the behavioural factors that influence how you can project yourself in more effective and pleasing ways, i.e. how to give yourself a new image.

Your Appearance

This, in all situations has a huge impact!

Approximately 90% of what people see of you are your clothes - so is their **visual impact** sufficiently pleasing and impressive? Do not appear dishevelled or sloppily dressed. In general, you should aim to achieve an understated elegance appropriate to the formal occasion. It is sometimes said that you should "dress to impress for success". But what exactly does this imply?, In the upper echelons of UK male society, by many, this is taken to mean:-

- A well-pressed, impeccably-fitting, buttoned-up, double-breasted, plain, dark suit. If you are short of stature, do not have turn-ups on your trousers.

- Well-polished, plain, lace-up leather shoes (with leather soles), and dark plain socks colour co-ordinated to your suit and possibly your tie.

- Plain white, cream or ivory coloured, double-cuffed (with non-ostentatious links) shirt, preferably without a breast pocket. Avoid the choice of a striped shirt (with a buttoned-down collar) on important occasions - the stripes tend to distract your audience, and can even physically upset migraine sufferers.

- An elegant, matt-finished, tightly-woven, plain silk-tie, tied in a half-Windsor knot.

- A subtle silk pocket-handkerchief of colour to match the tie.

- Wear comfortable clothes, not a brand-new outfit.

These recommendations indicate the current uppermost level of fashion for British business men, who wish to make the best of their appearance. The degree of haute couture adopted should depend upon what is likely to be expected by your audience for your forthcoming formal occasion. Some interviewers regard highly the confidence shown by those audacious enough to wear, for instance, a pretentious waistcoat, but, when in doubt, it is normally wiser to dress more conservatively. For some interviews, e.g. for junior research personnel, casual but clean clothing is sufficient.

Even with accoutrements there are many possible pitfalls. For example, for signing forms, etc, it is usually more dignified to employ a **fountain pen** rather than a ball-point pen. For all occasions, make certain the lenses of your spectacles are clean. When attending an interview, copies of your c.v. and letter of application, together with your well-ordered corroboratory transparencies and evidence, should be carried in a thin, dark-leather **briefcase.**

Body language: the silent speech-process

Many people who have been made redundant, after years in one organisation, soon lose self-confidence. This can be seen for instance by their shoulders slumping, heads not being held upright and harassed facial expressions (Young 1994). It almost appears as though they are ashamed of themselves and so trying to hide from society. Thus, if you are depressed, beware of inadvertently showing your true feelings. On important occasions, look alert with your adrenalin flowing sufficiently rapidly. The residual **visual** impression you leave with your audience is often more influential than the information you gave them.

Beware:- Shrugging shoulders often indicates indifference; clasping your arms around your chest signifies you are mentally unnerved; and rubbing your nose or tugging an ear reveals your puzzlement or bewilderment.

If the words convey one message, while non-verbal behaviour suggests another, the non-verbal message (e.g. speed, emphasis and tone of delivery, as well as body posture) will usually be the truer one. Thus, to achieve conviction, the two messages should reinforce one another: ie. your verbal message should be consistent with your body language.

How to develop "presence" and appear more authoritative

*   Approximately 80% of what we communicate to others is based on what our body language is conveying, i.e. silent-speech signals, so behave accordingly.

*   Body language is contagious: therefore, keep away from despondent people!

*   Practise walking purposefully, at a pace slightly faster than your colleagues, and refrain from looking down at the ground.

*   Think before you speak.

*   Act and speak with confidence. Decide in advance what you are going to do when a situation arises, and do it!

*   Avoid apologising too frequently - this is an entrenched habit of the British. Think positively. For instance, don't say "It's only a thought, but ...." or "I'd just like to suggest that ....".

*   Use a tape-recorder to listen to your own voice and subsequently assess it critically. Try to develop a more confident-sounding voice - speak slowly and tweak the pitch of your voice **downwards**.

- As an automatic habit, assess the likely subject matter of each proposed meeting well in advance: this will enable you to be more confident and so adjust your behaviour accordingly.

Practise improving your presence, when speaking in front of a full-length mirror, so that you can see not just your face but also your posture, stance and gestures. For instance, maintain eye contact with the mirror images of your eyes (which represent those of the person with whom you are simulating being in conversation). Practise winking or your "eye-brow flash" greetings : i.e. for the latter, when meeting someone, for a fifth of a second, raise and subsequently lower your eyebrows. This is friendly conversation without words.

When lecturing, don't "hide behind" your folded arms or a desk. Use expansive, open gestures of your arms; your palms being held upwards. Avoid distracting mannerisms, e.g. jingling coins in your pocket, fiddling with pens or chalk, as well as swaying from one foot to another. Look approachable, i.e. don't appear to take yourself too seriously.

To improve the empathy achieved with whoever you are speaking, practise TIME-LOCK, i.e. focus solely on the present task, so giving your complete attention to the person(s) you are with here and now (and temporarily ignore your worries emanating from the past or the future).

Effective Listening

'God has wisely given us two ears and one mouth, so that we may hear twice as much as we speak.' -(Epictitus-an ancient Greek philosopher)

As you develop your listening skills, you will interrupt less frequently and learn more.

Responsibility for achieving exact understanding is shared between the sender and the receiver of the communication. Thus effective **listening** is essential for two-way communication between the speaker and the listener: for example, asking pertinent questions, which should be encouraged, will help avoid ambiguities.

Your active **listeners** are not only receiving your words, but also registering your tone of voice, assessing your body language as well as making judgements on your manner and appearance. The members of a bored audience will tend to fidget, look at their watches, gaze at the floor or out of the window, and may even sigh noisily.

Resist distractions. Listen for ideas and for what is said, rather than for how it is said.

Hold your ego in check. Too often during important interviews or at meetings, we are inclined to be so concerned with what **we wish** to say next, that we miss vital points by not listening sufficiently well to what is being said by others. It is wiser to show visibly your interest in the conversation by smiling intermittently, with ears pricked up and, when in agreement, nodding your head affirmatively and leaning forward slightly. However, beware of fake half-hearted listening, i.e. when you are thinking of other things - you could then easily be embarrassed by being asked a detailed, unexpected question.

There are three modes of listening **actively**:-

(i)   In **diagnostic listening**, you act as a consultant trying to diagnose what needs to be done. Initially, you probe for symptoms while remaining non-judgmental, so not arousing the speaker's anxiousness. Is what is being stated in harmony with the body language employed? Is the speaker excessively anxious? Why? What is being hidden?

(ii)   **Reflective listening**. Regularly summarize aloud what has been said by the speaker: this should avoid misunderstandings arising and wasteful mistakes being propagated. If in doubt, ask.

(iii)   **Empathic listening**. Try to put yourself in the speaker's "shoes" in order to appreciate his/her perception of the situation.

Check list for effective listening.

Do you:-

• Look interested and have eye contact with the person speaking?

• Have a pen and paper ready to make notes when needed?

• Ask pertinent questions to clarify ambiguities, but avoid unnecessarily interrupting the speaker?

• Try to distinguish between facts and opinions in what is being propagated?

• Concentrate sufficiently well on what is being said and evaluate it with respect to what is in it for you?

• Prevent your prejudices distracting you from the content of the conversation?

• Avoid over-reacting to what the speaker says and thereby lose control of your thoughts and hence the train of the argument?

"CHECK FOR EFFECTIVE LISTENING"

4 SELF AND OTHER ADVERTISING

Job seeking

(See figure 2.2)

You must have a competitive edge. Do you look and act like someone worth employing to fill the advertised vacancy? To answer this question, you need a detailed awareness of your **corporate image**. How do you "come across"? Your low level of personal hygiene, excessive use of low-quality after-shave lotion, the tattiness of your c.v., your irritating voice, etc., can all contribute to having a negative impact and a perceived general languor of body and mind. If you act like a jaded "has-been" and don't look in control of yourself, what prospective employer will be interested in you? If you really want a better job, you should **now** be practising how to project yourself effectively in the best light, more or less continuously, i.e. long before any vitally important interview. You should **always** look and act the part you wish to play, ie: practise, practise, practise, ...

Wasted Effort: Do not squander your mental endeavours, applying for a job unless you are convinced that you possess exactly what the organisation wants, and that you have a unique value for them. For example, companies manufacturing, say, steam turbines are likely to have few vacancies for electronic engineers, and electronic firms, few vacancies for mechanical engineers.

Tactics

Regularly survey the job opportunities advertised in the press. When a sufficiently attractive job is advertised, for which you believe you are well qualified and in which you would flourish:-

* revise, if necessary, your well laid-out c.v. to emphasise your pertinent strengths.

* compose a well-focused, personalised letter of application: it should be clear, confident, well-expressed and designed to highlight how

your skills and experience match the requirements of the advertised job.

- complete with care an application form (if needed).

- submit several copies of this documentation to the person specified in the advertisement.

These four essential steps should help your candidature and so result in you being short-listed.

When seeking any appointment, you should try and put yourself in the prospective employer's shoes. His/her critical question, after reading your c.v. is "Would I wish to employ this candidate?" If not, you should redraft and improve it. Time spent in this way is usually an excellent investment. It is also wise to be aware of the persuasive techniques now employed, even by universities, when recruiting (e.g. see the section on 'Advertising undergraduate courses' in Chapter 4).

If you are seeking a "top" job, the lack of an answer-phone (at home) may lose you a crucial invitation to discuss a prospective opportunity.

Curriculum Vitae (c.v.)

A high-impact, well-presented (e.g. not cramped) c.v. is usually an essential ever-ready document for a successful career. It should be typed on one side only of an A4 sheet: more detailed information (e.g. a list of your publications) can, if necessary, be presented in appendices to the c.v. It should be laser printed and neatly laid-out with plenty of white space (which can be used for annotations by the interviewer). Be succinct and always positive. Don't waffle or employ unusual abbreviations.

The c.v. should be a **factual** document, (i.e. not containing any opinions), presenting chronologically the highlights of your career, describing accurately your experiences and main responsibilities as well as listing your home and office telephone numbers. Do not be diffident about disclosing your successes. It should also give the names, addresses and telephone numbers of at least two referees,* with whom you have had recent contact in your professional career, and who **actively** wish to support your career enhancement.

In the intensifying competition for the more rewarding jobs, there are increasing temptations to be "economical with the truth" - see Table 1.

TRUTH	AS STATED IN C.V.
grape picker in France	wine supplier
washed dishes in a ski-resort bar	catering support-manager
in prison, "at her Majesty's pleasure"	freelance security-consultant
sewed mail bags	worked for the Post Office

TABLE 1.   The truth and what has appeared in c.v.s.

Beware of misleading statements or bogus claims for qualifications - they are easily detected by professional interviewers. A survey of accountancy companies concluded that at least half of the candidates interviewed made false statements on their c.v.s. Other complaints included incorrect spelling, poor presentation and undesirable information about (irresponsible) hobbies, political leanings and religious beliefs.

*Footnote. Be aware, however, that legal experts now advise that the words "without legal responsibility" are added, to all references supplied by employers, to ensure that they cannot be sued for negligence concerning the statements made therein.

Your Sales Document

1. Your **'curriculum vitae'**, i.e. a 'study of your life', is one of the most important documents that you need in the process of job hunting.

a) It should be an up-to-date and clear statement of what you have accomplished.

b) Thereby, you provide yourself with a readily-available and complete record of your important achievements, together with the pertinent dates and places.

c) So, it makes: (i) job-application form filling easier and usually more accurate
and (ii) writing a letter of application and preparing for an interview more systematic and easier.

d) It should depict you as you would wish to be perceived.

e) It can be used, without embarrassment, to remind friends, employers, referees, guarantors and relatives of your accomplishments, e.g. if there is a likelihood that they will be approached to vouch for you.

2. **Compiling your c.v.**

a) Write out the important items of your career record - education, prizes, awards, jobs, etc., as they come to mind.

b) List the best examples of your accomplishments.

c) Make a personal evaluation of yourself. List your strengths while being aware of your weaknesses, so as to arrive at your **useful selling points**.

d) Try to make sure you have an 'end product' to most paragraphs, i.e. show what **you** achieved.

e) Arrange the information in chronological order, stating the appropriate dates (e.g. year of birth rather than how old you are now).

f) It is sound policy to attach a passport sized photograph to the top right-hand corner of your c.v. (Interviewers are mere mortals and tend to forget details - a photograph does aid their powers of recall when they are writing up their summaries). Do not let them forget **YOU.**

g) Be sparing and careful with words. Remember, nowadays, at the first stage of sifting through, say, more than one hundred applications for the job, your c.v. may be scanned (by a computer) to see whether it contains the key words that describe the appointment.

h) **You** must shine through: make the c.v. live, so the reader will probably say: "This person I must see".

3.   The use of your c.v.

a) Do not attach your c.v. to a first letter in response to an advertisement, unless requested to do so.

b) If you are making a general enquiry in the hope of being invited to an interview, but no vacancies have been advertised, submit it with your letter.

c) Attach it to your application form (ensuring it cannot become detached), if the requested information for the form does not allow **YOU** to "shine" .

4. Skeleton of a c.v. with notes on each section.

a)	NAME	FORENAMES
b)	NATIONALITY	When applying for a job abroad, ensure that you have a work permit for that country, and a right of residence there.
c)	AGE	If an advertisement specifies a young graduate, it generally follows that they are not prepared to pay very much or they require a trainee.
d)	MARRIED/SINGLE*	Married men are often unfairly looked upon as more stable.
	CHILDREN*	Married men or women with children are usually loath to be relocated many times.
e)	PREVIOUS STUDIES	Nature of study; where; when; course and content, thesis or dissertation or project work, title?
f)	CURRENT STUDIES	What course are you on? Thesis topic? Why did you choose this? What do you hope to gain?
g)	EXPERIENCE	Training? Engineering design? Sales? Development? Research? Marketing? Level of responsibility?
		Vacation work - was it relevant? Industrial placements? What did you gain?
h)	PROFESSIONAL QUALIFICATIONS	Are you a member or are you seeking membership of a professional institution?

*Footnote. Equal Opportunities Legistlation (Sex Discrimination Act 1975) means that employers should not normally raise or consider marital status or children as issues of employment.

Written Applications for Jobs

Suggestions

Analyse the advertisement and any other information concerning the job. Break it down under two headings:

    (i) The job content   - purpose
                                             - responsibility

    (ii) Personal requirements - specialist knowledge
                                               - qualifications
                                             - experience
                                             - age

Your short, polite letter of application is aimed at interesting the advertiser (usually the personnel/staff/training officer) in YOU.

- At this stage, YOU are trying initially to get an interview, rather than the job. At the subsequent **interview**, YOU are trying to get <u>THE JOB</u>.

- In endeavouring to interest the members of the short-listing panel, match your experience and qualifications against your interpretation of the ideal man-profile for the job. Remember - your prospective employer has probably invested a great deal of thought in devising the advertisement and therefore knows exactly what s(he) wants.

- Be aware that probably all that the short-listing panel will know about you is derived from what they read in your application and c.v. Therefore, ensure that your letter is set out attractively, legible, preferably typed and well paragraphed. Untidiness will convey sloppiness or a lack of motivation.

- Avoid submitting a c.v. with only a business card attached or a photocopied generalised covering letter: such a casual approach suggests a lack of sufficient desire to obtain this job.

- Keep a copy of your letter. You might be asked to complete an application form (a necessary chore for 9 out of 10 jobs) and you will want your letter and form to be consistent in emphasis on relevant experience.

*   Whatever you say, make sure it is accurate. Most firms will check with referees or authorities regarding the authenticity of your information before they **offer** you the job.

*   Address the advertiser as 'Dear Sir/Madam', unless his/her name appears in the advertisement. In the former case, you should end your letter "Yours faithfully,.........."
    and in the latter case with "Yours sincerely,..............".

*   In your first letter do not tell the advertiser **everything** about yourself, but provide sufficient relevant information to whet his/her appetite for more. (You will have opportunities at subsequent interviews!).

*   Don't mention salary in your first letter.

*   Do not make your first letter an autobiography; keep it down to one page if you can.

*   Check it for errors, omissions and punctuation.

Speculative letters

Make a list of the companies for which you would like to work. (This may require you consulting Kompass, Key British Enterprises, or other reference books in your local library). Remember, many excellent firms do not formally advertise for staff, but rely on a network of contacts when recruiting. Nevertheless, in such a case, a proactive, direct approach from you can lead to a significant opportunity arising. Some firms welcome such initiative and respond encouragingly.

However, do:-

*   make sure that you are projecting yourself in a receptive market.

*   ensure that it is probable that your background and professional discipline will appeal to the firm.

*   where **possible**, approach the Managing Director rather than the Personnel Officer.

Advertising Undergraduate Courses

You cannot judge a college solely by its prospectus, any more than you can tell what a holiday will be like from a brochure. Some advertisements deserve to have appended to them "This course could be damaging to your mental health".

The following comments are based on the survey by Dr Frederick Volkmann, Vice-Chancellor for Public Affairs, Washington University, St Louis, USA, but amplified to take into account some British experiences. The means, assessed according to the number of suitable students recruited per pound sterling expended, are ranked as follows; the most effective being the first in the list:-

1. One-to-one, face-to-face conversation with an appropriately-qualified academic or an enthusiastic previous graduate of the university, who clearly states the benefits of undertaking the course, and describes it accurately. S(he) should "press the flesh" of the candidate.

2. Small group discussion with such an academic or graduate.

3. Either of these persuasive, committed advocates speaking before a large carefully-targeted audience.

4. A telephone conversation with the staff member or graduate, e.g. who should emphasise (i) how British society has vastly underestimated the percentage of the population that could greatly enrich their lives by university-level education; (ii) you do not have to be exceptionally intelligent or wealthy to benefit from a university course; (iii) various sources of financial support are available; and (iv) the application form is simple to complete.

5. **Hand-written** relevant personal letter from the academic staff member, in a stamped (not franked) hand-written envelope, preferably using the first name of the prospective recruit. The envelope should not be crumpled, and the stuck-on stamps not skew-whiff on the envelope.

6. Typewritten, but personal letter from the academic - not a word-processor generated note. It should be individually but legibly signed rather than having a signature generated by a word processor: the signature is the first item read by most readers.

7. Computer-generated "personal" letter from the academic staff member. It should leave sufficient "white space" for introducing annotations by the reader. The use of **sub-headings** and words or phrases in italics (or underlined) to attract attention usually makes a document more easily comprehended.

8. Mass-produced non-personal letter.

9. Pamphlet targeted at the prospective applicant. However good the educational course you are selling, the sales literature must hold your prospective students' attention: it should help them in making an aspiration come true. Thus it needs persuasive headlines indicating substantial benefits: it should create desire by stating, with supporting evidence, why it is better than other nominally similar courses. Why is it unique? Guarantee whatever you can. Give the applicant good reasons why to apply now and minimize the admissions bureaucracy.

10. Glossy brochure sent out by direct mail (e.g. to head masters of schools).

11. Advertisement on an appropriate notice board.

12. Article in a university newsletter.

13. Advertisements via newspapers/radio/t.v. These tend to be relatively expensive and many doubt the desirability of spending so much of the state-provided budget for education in this way. There is an approximate inverse correlation between the quality of the university education provided and the cost of such prolific advertising emanating from that university. In general, it is wise to offer neither judgements nor opinions in advertisements, but rather to state unambiguous facts. The recent trend of making exaggerated, anti-social claims is unethical. A free post or free phone service for encouraging personal enquiries is desirable.

Usually, mass mail-drops give the recruiter the belief that s(he) is working hard, doing something useful. But the effectiveness of such procedures is increasingly questioned by the findings of unbiased cost/benefit analyses.

5 INTERVIEWS

The right (wo)man for the job?

Traditionally, a short list of suitable candidates is interviewed, with the intention of appointing the best of them to join a team. Generally, it is wise to select the most SUITABLE candidate rather than the most ELIGIBLE - see Table 1. Past achievements indicate eligibility, whereas future performance is usually dictated more by the suitability of the person chosen. Also how well the job is done is more important than how well-qualified is the person doing it. Unfortunately, many occupy jobs for which they are well-qualified, but which they perform poorly, i.e. the Peter Principle.

Table 1. Guide for better selection (after Meredith Belbin)

Normal Entry Criteria	Actual Performance Criteria
Qualifications	Aptitude/Ability to understand problems
Relevant experience	Versatility of behaviour
Effusive written references	Assessments (e.g. psychometric)
Excellent interview performance	Ability to fit in with the team

Success at Interviews: From the employer's perspective:-

Those organisations, which are well-skilled in selecting personnel for senior appointments, may not rely solely on formal correspondence and interviews. For these bodies, the assessment of each candidate may take over two days and use a mixture of techniques such as psychometric tests and group discussions (see Cohen, 1993). For instance, in appointing a university professor, it would be wise if each of the short-listed candidates were required to lecture, for one hour, to students and staff, on a subject of the candidate's choice. Other job-simulation exercises should be devised, in order to be able to predict better how each candidate would perform if appointed: this would allow the candidate to show what s(he) could bring to the job. Nevertheless, the interview remains an important part of the selection process.

The key to good interviewing, as with most things in life, is thorough **preparation.** Yet too often, this is skimped. It is also essential that equality of opportunity ensues throughout the recruitment process. Beware of being aggressive, talking too much and making up your mind prematurely.

Prior to the interview, the following should be considered:-

- **Prepare** a detailed job description and hence a specification for the most-suitable person required to undertake the job, listing the desired attributes/skills in the sought-after candidate. Are you seeking a replacement or someone with different/additional skills?

- **Prepare** the job advertisement, specifying accurately what is required, and ensure that it is published appropriately (e.g. with the desired impact in newspapers likely to be read by the ideal candidate).

- As a result of studying beforehand all the available information (e.g. profile of desired person, the letters of application, c.v.s and knowledge gleaned from telephone conversations about the short-listed candidates), **prepare** a list of searching questions, to be posed to the candidates during the interview. With other members of the interview committee, decide well in advance of the interview which member is going to lead in probing each aspect of the applicant's idiosyncrasies.

- **Prepare** and issue an individual timetable for each short-listed applicant, so that there is no possibility of the other candidates waiting simultaneously in the same room. Anxiousness is contagious!

The interview of each candidate and subsequent appointment procedure should have a pre-determined (but sensitive and flexible) structure:-

- In the interview room, introduce the members of the interview panel individually, stating their roles, to each candidate - see Appendix 5.1.

Allow the candidate time, if s(he) so wishes to note down the names of the members of the interview panel.

- Initially one should endeavour (via comments or questions, e.g. relating to travel arrangements that day) to put the candidate at his/her ease. Establish a good rapport and a relaxed atmosphere free from interruptions (e.g. telephone calls). Refrain from asking difficult or probing questions until the candidate is well settled. The interview should not be rushed.

- The use of "in-house" abbreviations or esoteric jargon should be avoided during interviews: the candidate may not be familiar with these terms and their use then would tend to make him/her feel uncomfortable.

- Listen to what each candidate says and note any gaps in his/her career description. It is unwise here to interrupt, criticise, make moral judgements or express your own opinions. However, there may be no certain way of differentiating fact from fiction at an interview. Nevertheless, to try to achieve this, it is sometimes necessary to ask straight, even blunt, questions. For example, if the candidate is obfuscating rather than replying clearly, it would be reasonable to ask "Would you be more specific about that?" or "I can't help noticing that you are avoiding this topic". In cases of prevailing doubt, it would be desirable to follow up references very thoroughly, after the interview, provided you are still interested in the candidate.

- After explaining the requirements which will be imposed on the person appointed, ask each candidate 'How would you satisfy these needs?'

- The purpose of the questions posed to the interviewee is to provide additional information to supplement or clarify what has already been submitted by the candidate. However, interviewers must avoid asking questions which can be construed as being discriminatory, e.g. about religious or political views, marital status, occupation of spouse, family intentions or domestic responsibilities. (Thus it is desirable that you are familiar, for instance, with the main tenets of the Equal Opportunities legislation **before** you act as an interviewer).

- Try to ask your questions at an appropriate time, by following the interviewee's lead, while discouraging rambling or irrelevant responses. However, it is desirable simultaneously to control the course of the interview so as not to stray too far from the pre-determined sequence of topics to be explored.

- Endeavour to ensure that the interviewee does the majority of the talking by asking only open-ended questions (i.e. those which cannot be answered by a simple 'yes' or 'no').

- Leading questions, i.e. those so phrased that the candidate realises what sort of answer the interviewer would prefer, should not be posed.

- Detect anxiety in the person you are interviewing by observing the small, sub consciously controlled movements of the hands and feet.

- Liars betray themselves in several ways - e.g. their body-language, such as rubbing of their hands, pulling or stroking their ears, nose or cheeks; or aggressive gestures.

- Likewise, the interviewee can detect boredom by an interviewer folding his/her arms, leaning away or refusing to return eye-contact.

- At the **end of each interview**, thank the candidate for attending. Each interviewee should leave feeling that s(he) has received a fair hearing and would like to work for your organisation. Remember: a disgruntled interviewee could be a bad advertisement.

- Your organisation should consider using a comprehensive, structured, well-tried assessment form for recording your comments regarding each candidate's relevant knowledge, confidence, personality, etc. This form should be completed by each interviewer (before meeting the next candidate), i.e. while your impressions are still fresh, and should indicate the demonstrated attributes of the character of each interviewee, especially noting the strong and weak points. These can be compared subsequently with each of the criteria laid down in the wo(man) profile for the job. This procedure will assist in achieving objectivity in the decision-making process. (N.B. Industrial Tribunals could ask for such records, as well as the Chairperson's notes, should a complaint of discrimination be made subsequently.)

- Beware of the grumbling interviewee: recall Aesop's aphorism in the mid-6th century BC: "*He that is discontented in one place will seldom be content in another*".

- Compare your conclusions with those of other members of the panel **only when all the interviews have been completed.** Do not necessarily make an immediate decision, but it should not be delayed excessively. Remember: all interviewers have personal biases - recognize your own and so make due allowances when arriving at your judgements.

- Take up references, for the three most preferred candidates, from the persons to whom the candidate reported in his/her two previous appointments.

- Come to a **consensus** decision as to who to appoint, subject to taking up final references. Explain, to the preferred candidate, that this will entail contacting their current employer once s(he) has told that employer. You can do this over the phone and ask "How would you rate the candidate's technical/time management/interpersonal/super-visory and management skills? Is there anything else you believe I should know?"

- Notify, as soon as is feasible, the successful candidate and all the other applicants. It is professionally irresponsible not to inform, in writing, the applicants who failed: a few words of encouragement in these letters are well worthwhile, e.g., you might state that, if the candidate so wishes, his/her personal details will be kept on file ready for consideration for future appointments.

Conducting interviews properly is time consuming. However, if wrong choices are made, or the appointed person resigns soon after appointment, large costs could be incurred, and much effort wasted. Thus the recruiter should, throughout the selection process be asking "Can and will the interviewee cope with the job, and how well will s(he) do it?"

Success at Interviews: From the candidate's viewpoint

"No one can make you feel inferior without your consent." - ***Eleanor Roosevelt (1884-1962)***

You have been invited for an interview. Congratulations - your c.v. and letter of application were obviously sufficiently well-prepared that you have been successful at marketing yourself **on paper**. You must now be equally convincing **in person**. Be positive. Sell yourself!
If feasible, subject yourself to a mock interview in front of friends or colleagues.

Ensure you are always punctual. Try to arrive the previous day within the locality where the interview is to be held. (If you travel a long distance on the day of the interview, you will possibly be tired on arrival as a result of the journey. Also there is the risk of being late, or even missing the interview, because, for instance, of your car breaking down or a train delay). Do a meticulous recce to familiarize yourself with the neighbourhood and determine **exactly** where the interview is to be held. Is there adequate car parking close by? Return to your hotel, enjoy a good meal and retire to bed early.

Don't carry your personal phone around with you (and especially not into the interview room).

Check that you have copies of your completed application form and c.v. with you. Plan to arrive, without rushing, at the rendezvous for the interview about 30 minutes before the stated time. This gives you ample time to relax.

During the wait preceding the interview, prepare yourself psychologically. Concentrate solely on this occasion and calm yourself using a meditation routine (see Chapter 10). Practise time-lock: try to dispel all worries emerging from the past, eliminate the fear of failure and avoid the burden of excessive expectation.

As you are likely to be nervous, it is wise **not** to accept a cup of tea or coffee immediately before (or during) the interview. Not only does a rattling cup and saucer betray your nervousness, there is the increased possibility that you could have an embarrassing spillage with a temporary disastrous effect on your self-esteem.

Remember that the opinions of those you meet before and after the interview may well be sought by the appointing committee - so be polite throughout the day.

Before being summoned into the interview room, check you have a small notebook available in which to jot down the names of the interviewers, ideas, comments, etc., during the interview, with a properly functioning fountain-pen, recently recharged with a new ink-cartridge.

First (and last) impressions tend to be lasting impressions, so it is wise to "get them right". From the first 30 seconds of a meeting, those around you will glean vital information concerning your:- appearance; levels of confidence; competence; sincerity; trustworthiness; as well as social background. Thus it is wise to practise at least the first few minutes of the forthcoming interview, perhaps with the help of a camcorder and a critical friend.

Enter the interview room with purpose and confidence - you must look successful. Immediately, the chairperson of the committee will introduce you to its members. Stretch out your right hand, with your palm vertical, to each of the interviewers in turn. Yours should be a firm (web-to-web) but gentle, friendly, confident handshake with each interviewer immediately in front of you: simultaneously you should **smile**, deliver a courteous greeting and maintain eye contact. Assure the interviewers by your behaviour that you are well-used to coping with this sort of stressful situation. Remember you do not get a second chance at making a good first impression. How long does it take for an interviewee to make his/her mark? - a short time if someone is weak, but much longer to show s(he) should be appointed.

Wait to be invited to sit down - where will be indicated. When you do so, do not slouch - always display good posture and look alert. The chairperson will then engage you in various pleasantries (e.g. about your

43

journey or your university) to help establish a rapport. However, do not unbend your mind too much, despite your wish to appear relaxed. You should aim to convey throughout the interview, your:-

- commitment and competence.

- vigour (i.e. stamina to go the whole duration of the appointment).

- professionalism and trustworthiness.

Never emit signals (e.g. by facial expressions) showing that you feel inferior to any member of the interview committee: treat them as professional equals. If this is difficult for you, imagine them all naked, sitting on water-closets around the interview table - this tends to help make you feel less overawed by the occasion. Refuse to be intimidated! Believe you will succeed and that you are only there to dot the "i"s and cross the "t"s: your superb written application has already almost won the battle. Take a deep breath each time you feel nervous. Treat the interview as part of your education, or as you would a game of chess - it is not a "life or death" threatening situation.

- Speak clearly and deliberately, simultaneously using gestures with open hands, palms upward. Count up to ten mentally before answering any question. In your heightened mental-stress situation, what may appear to you to be speaking slowly will probably be perceived by your listeners as occurring at normal speed.

- You need to think well in advance of the interview, as well as during it, about the content and style of what you wish to say. Like politicians, you should use sound bites: you only have a relatively short time to influence the interviewers, so be succinct.

- Look serious, credible and unflappable: an occasional **smile** at an appropriate moment helps enormously in conveying a confident image.

Remind yourself to use positive **body-language** and a positive posture (see Chapter 3) throughout the interview. An abbreviated check list is:-

- Sit upright (with your spine leaning slightly forward from the vertical) and look alert.

- Avoid crossing your arms or your legs, and putting your hands to your head, for instance to either rub your nose, tug your ear lobes, cover your mouth or tousle your hair. Avoid clicking your pen or tapping it on, say, the table in front of you.

- Always face, and have intermittent **eye-contact** with whichever of your interviewers is speaking or with someone you are striving to impress - but do not stare at him/her. Three to six seconds eye contact is recommended: anything less may appear shifty. Show interest in what s(he) is saying. Break eye contact **downwards:** movement **sideways** suggests boredom and **upwards** scepticism.

Try to steer the discussion to your strengths and achievements. Emphasise you will fit in, your coolness when under high stress and capability of dealing with difficult situations. Nevertheless, you have to **give the interviewers what they want to know** rather than always what you want to tell them. You are there to sell yourself with modesty, confidence, calmness **and** neither to be too pushy nor to beg. Establish your credibility and suitability during the interview. There should be a strong main theme running throughout your performance, e.g. emphasise your financial viability and/or academic responsibility/respectability. Be friendly, polite and positive. Hence the need for excellent prior preparation, e.g. researching the present and future prospects for the organisation that is interviewing you. It should then be easier to convince the interviewing panel that you do fit the forthcoming vacancy. Be enthusiastic without going overboard. Try, by giving examples from your career, to indicate your relevant strengths, e.g. that you are well organised, can keep several projects progressing simultaneously and are well able to deal effectively with difficult people. Try always to be positive (especially about yourself) rather than negative! Always use positive language! Never answer the question "How are you?" with "Not bad", "Could be better", "Awful", "Dreadful" or even "Fine". Banish negativity from your vocabulary.

However provoked, maintain your composure! Do not become flustered by awkward questions. If necessary, ask questions to clarify those posed by the interviewers. If you don't know the answer, admit it, but this should rarely be so. Undoubtedly, you will be asked some searching questions. Some anticipated inquiries could be:-

- Why do you wish to leave your present job? (It is wise to be positive about your existing employment.)

- Why do you wish to work for this company?
  (i) You are interested in their products.
  (ii) Their reputation is excellent.
  (iii) You like its location, e.g. it is near your home.

- Why should we appoint you? ("As can be seen from my c.v., I have been preparing systematically for this job over the last decade. I have done....")

- How will this organisation benefit by employing you?

- What aspects of the job appeal to you most and least?

- How would you describe yourself?

- Describe a situation in which you showed considerable initiative.

- What was most rewarding about your work last year?

- What are your main strengths and weaknesses?

- What has been your most embarrassing situation at work?

- What major mistakes have you made that have affected your career?

Succinct honest replies to such questions can be rehearsed thoroughly, well ahead of the interview. Answer the questions as though the interviewing panel knows nothing about you, apart from what has been presented in your c.v. and letter of application. Be prepared to substantiate anything stated therein. You need to be very clear why you want the job and **what you can offer**. Show the organisation how well you would complement the exiting team. Keep your answers logical and to the point. Neither monosyllabic responses nor interminable waffle will advance your cause. As mentioned previously, never rush to answer a question - even though you have a well-prepared reply. Have clear independent views of the issues raised, and hold to those views by the use of confident, articulate, assured arguments. Never speak ill of another or disparage any previous colleagues or employers. Remember: *"A man never describes his own character so clearly as when he describes another" - Jean-Paul Richter, German satirist (1763-1825).*

In addition, at the interview: -

- Avoid **emphasising** your involvements with dangerous sports or excessive spare-time commitments (e.g. watching t.v.).

- Don't proffer your opinions regarding sex, politics or religion - with these subjects, it is too easy to offend an interviewer.

Occasionally during a panel interview, one member will "switch off", once s(he) has asked her/his questions. Nevertheless, keep intermittent eye contact with all the members of the panel, even if one is wriggling in his/her seat or yawning. You, as a candidate, should try to keep them all in the conversation by comments like "Dr Einstein (i.e. the sleeping panellist) earlier quite rightly stated that .....". You need each of their votes. Display impeccable manners throughout.

Part of the technique of impressing the interviewers is to show that you have assessed the demands of the job. You should have taken previous opportunities to try to clarify anything ambiguous about the supplied background information. Therefore, you should have some well-constructed, informed, searching questions to ask the committee at appropriate opportunities during the interview. For instance, if up for appointment as an engineering professor, you might inquire as to "Why was the Engineering Department of the University last year in such a healthy financial surplus?" or "What happened to the person occupying this position previously?" However, beware of asking a question that embarrasses the committee or has already been answered earlier in the interview. If you have not already done so, ask to be allowed to meet those with whom you would be working most closely if appointed.

Final impressions are also vitally important. Try to leave on a high positive note without the interview fizzling out. Shake hands with all the members of the committee. Thank them for (i) short-listing you, (ii) the interesting challenge that the interview itself has imposed for you and (iii) the hospitality received. This helps keep the "chemistry" right between you and the panel.

Conduct a postmortem with yourself immediately after the interview. Ask yourself:-

• What went well or poorly during the interview?

• What questions and answers were the interviewers most interested in and why?

• Did I (i) speak too quickly or mumble, (ii) waffle or (iii) drift off the point?

It is desirable that you should feel that you have gained significantly (with respect to understanding your strengths and weaknesses) as a result of being interviewed, rather than having wasted one or more days. Even if you are unsuccessful this time, as a post-interview action, request feedback as to why you were not appointed. Any constructive comments received should help with preparations for future interviews. The prospective employer during the interview probably will have probed whether your qualifications and experience were relevant to the proposed job. It is wise now to do a reassessment of this. However, you should remember your personality was also being judged with respect to demonstrating:-

- an enthusiastic positive 'can-do' behaviour pattern

- creative ideas and problem-solving skills

- confidence to inspire and lead

- a self-awareness of your strengths and weaknesses

- an open mind to new ideas, and a willingness to learn

- your effectiveness at communicating

Remember that it is impossible for any one to be the perfect interviewee.

Being interviewed live 'on the radio'

- Treat the occasion as though you are only speaking with the interviewer (e.g. as if you were on the telephone).

- Sit comfortably without slouching.

- Speak clearly into the microphone - gestures go unnoticed in this context - your body language won't be of any help to you.

- Having done your homework about the subject of the interview, you should be confident. Have a list of essential points you wish to make, written out and edited several times.

- Be succinct but thorough and comprehensive, while selecting your words with special care. Have well-rehearsed "sound bites".

- Your written notes should be on cue cards rather than on sheets of paper, whose rustling can be very disturbing when detected by the microphone. See also Chaper 8.

- Speak at a moderate pace: 'gabbling' suggests nervousness, whereas speaking very slowly will result in losing your listeners' attention.

Being interviewed live on television

- Dress soberly: a highly-patterned shirt and/or tie will divert your audience's attention from your face. It is preferable, for men, to use a pastel coloured (rather than a bright white) shirt, and, for women, plain clothes.

- It is wiser to avoid wearing spectacles, but if you have to, employ lenses with non-reflecting (i.e. ¼ wavelength) coatings.

- Try to be located against a static, plain background, so that you hold the viewers' attention.

- Ensure that you are well positioned relative to the lighting, so that it is flattering to you.

- Don't be put off by the presence of the T.V. camera. Think of its lens as a single, friendly interviewer.

- During the interview, avoid being self-conscious - e.g. forget about your appearance.

- Act naturally (e.g. with respect to your voice or accent) as otherwise you will appear false.

- Do not over-gesticulate: stand or sit still, and avoid fidgeting.

APPENDIX 5.1 - HOW TO INTRODUCE PEOPLE:-

- **To the person accorded the most respect,** present the other. The hierarchy of respect in such circumstances is:-

  (i)   rank (e.g. Head of the Church, or prospective employer);
  (ii)   women (before men);
  (iii)   the elder person.

- A seated woman rises for a man only if (i) she is the host or (ii) his rank takes precedence.

- A man shakes hands with a woman, only if the woman stretches forth her hand first.

- What to say: "Mr/Mrs/Ms (top-rank person's name), I would like to present (name of the lower person in hierarchy list)". There follows 'How do you do?' in formal situations, or 'How are you?' or 'Pleased to meet you' (even when it may not be so - as in an admonitory interview). It is important not to mumble, but to be clearly audible.

- First names should be used amongst friends. This is normally initiated by the person who is older or superior in rank. Do not reciprocate unless you are invited to do so.

6   *MEETINGS*

Is your meeting really necessary?

- Travelling to and from meetings can be highly expensive both in time and money. Thus, is the get-together necessary to achieve one of your high-priority objectives? Even if a face-to-face meeting is deemed essential, a prior exchange of views by telephone or fax can either make the meeting more productive, or eliminate its need. Sometimes, "at meetings, minutes are taken, but hours are wasted". There is often much truth in this facetious remark.

- Stick to the agenda. Poorly-managed meetings can be costly, time-wasting and boring. However, with an effective chairperson, an efficient secretary and appropriately-qualified members, a meeting can harness a range of skills and professional experience to help solve quickly a difficult problem or make a decision in a democratic way.

- You should not have a meeting costing £1000 to solve a £100 problem. Always be aware of the costs of holding a meeting (e.g. for hiring a room as well as for the time of those attending).

Suggestions for improving effectiveness

- **Punctuality**: Some people regularly compel you to wait to try to indicate their dominance over you. After 15 minutes waiting for a meeting to start (during which you should ensure that you have worked profitably on your own), you should request that the meeting be rearranged for some mutually more convenient time.

- In order to reduce wastages of time and effort, the **first** item of the Agenda for any committee meeting should be 'Any Urgent Business' (AUB). Also, no item should be included on the Agenda unless it is likely to lead to a worthwhile decision or an action.

- To avoid having protracted, low-productivity per hour expended, committee meetings, it is sometimes wise **not** to include an 'Any Other Business' (AOB) item on the Agenda.

- Avoid any discussion becoming unfocused: this can easily happen if there is no clear objective, or if there are too many participants.

- It is interesting to note that all UK Privy Council meetings are held with its members standing up, presumably as a recipe for achieving succinctness.

- The knowledge that the proceedings of a meeting are being tape-recorded can often act as a deterrent, so reducing the loquaciousness of otherwise verbose speakers.

- Throughout the meeting, try to concentrate creatively; if neccessary, attack issues, but never individuals.

- Research the answers to likely difficult questions. Practise using phrases that both make you sound knowledgeable, and help pull the disparate thoughts of the meeting together.

- Remain polite and friendly throughout.

- If you feel liked and respected, you will speak with greater confidence and authority. Therefore develop your interpersonal skills.

- Keep your "cool" at meetings. If you realise you are about to lose your temper, just say "I can't discuss this rationally now. Let me think about it, and we will talk later". Then go for a walk, calm down and subsequently review the situation. In so doing, try to improve the logic of your argument, rather than have the need to raise your voice in order to capture the attention of the people present. Remember: *"Interpret bad temper as a sign of inferiority"* - **Alfred Adler, Austrian psychiatrist (1870-1937.)**

- Responsibility for achieving exact understanding is shared between the sender and the receiver of the communication. Thus effective **listening** is essential (- see Chapter 3), as well as two-way communications between the speaker and the listener: for example, pertinent questions, which should be encouraged, help avoid ambiguities.

- **Tactics:** at meetings, let your colleagues present their views first, and only when the discussion is nearing exhaustion, introduce your opinions. These are then much more likely to be accepted than if you had thrust them forward initially.

- Rather than composing a traditional set of minutes of a committee meeting, it is usually preferable to produce a list of desired actions, with an indication of who is responsible for each of these actions being implemented within a stated timescale.

Negotiations

You will not succeed in work or life without being able to negotiate effectively. In business, you usually don't attain what you deserve, but rather what you are able to negotiate.

An important type of meeting ensues when you have to bargain to try to achieve your objective. The individuals involved often have different perceptions and differing vested interests concerning this goal. Nevertheless, a consensus approach is needed for progress to be achieved. Yet you may be highly reluctant to become involved in this communication situation because of:-

- Inadequate preparation. (It is wise to know your lowest acceptable terms of agreement and aim higher).

- Fear of failure. (But if you don't try, you will rarely win).

- Not wishing to become unpopular. (However, defending your own interests in an intelligent and dignified manner will earn you respect).

- The unease at possibly appearing selfish. (This is usually an emotional rather than rational fear).

- Your embarrassment at making a fuss. (But bringing the problem to the attention of the person, who has the power to make the necessary decision, is often well worthwhile).

To win at negotiations:-

AVOID	DO
◆ waffling	◆ listen carefully
◆ exaggerating	◆ frequently summarize the argument to date
◆ using sarcasm	◆ speak calmly, without raising your voice
◆ becoming emotional, e.g. blaming or threatening	◆ be diplomatic

7   REPORT WRITING

*"If any man wishes to write in a clear style, let him first be clear in his thoughts". - **Johann Wolfgang von Goethe, German author (1749-1832)**.*

The Problem

Unfortunately, inexactness, ambiguities and the misuse of words spill over from our domestic lives into our engineering and scientific communications. Consider, for example, what is normally referred to as a 'steam trap': what in practice this device achieves is to trap the condensate, while permitting the steam to flow through it. Similarly, an 'eye dropper' does not drop eyes and, in a 'nervous breakdown', nerves do not break. A 'wind generator' does not produce wind, but rather electricity, which has been converted from the wind-power harnessed by the turbine. Likewise, the commonly-used term 'thermal-insulation losses' refers to the heat passing through the insulant rather than, as implied, to losses of the insulant material. What we commonly mean by energy conservation is energy thrift or the rational use of energy: energy is automatically conserved according to the first law of thermodynamics. Certain so-called 'laws' are definitions, and so cannot be refuted experimentally, e.g. Ohm's law defines electrical resistance and Newton's laws of motion define force. However, by the careful choice and use of language, you should ensure that you cannot be misconstrued.

Effective, persuasive communications and exact understanding are vital for engineers - see for instance Appendix 7.1. Engineers are nevertheless notorious with respect to their poor presentational skills, regarding themselves primarily as doers rather than talkers about doing. However, other people's lives and their wealth are often the responsibilities of engineers, who thus have an implied professional duty to be exact communicators. While we fully recognise that even a comma in the wrong place in a computer program can have a catastrophic effect, such a strict adherence to punctuation correctness in a technical report is now, too often, absent.

Preliminary Advice

Numerous books discuss report writing in detail (e.g. see Maunder and Probert, 1972), and so the subject will not be laboured here. Suffice that a few important points will be reiterated.

- On starting your project, undertake a computer search, via twelve key words describing the project's aims, of the world's pertinent literature to ensure you are not attempting to "re-invent the wheel", i.e. that a truly worthwhile problem is being tackled. Also, at an early stage, write out a detailed target specification and realistic rolling-plan schedule (including deadlines) for the investigation.

- Do you suffer from writer's block? Do you find it extremely difficult to compose the company report, or a sales proposal? It is desirable to keep your composure under such circumstances. Try using a tape-recorder and speaking aloud your thoughts about the task in hand. Play the tape-recording back, and fit your recorded words on paper under appropriate headings.

- For scientists and engineers, all the likely-to-be-needed information, measurements, actions, relevant ideas and references for a subsequently-written report should be recorded immediately in an **information diary, wherever you are**. Note down appropriate phrases/ sentences/paragraphs: the right turns of phrase or exact succinct descriptions may occur to you at inconvenient times and are easily forgotten, so always have a pen and paper available, even in the bathroom. The resulting continual writing of such contributions in your diary, from the earliest stage in the project will form the base upon which your final report is constructed.

Report-writing methodology

Isolate yourself in a quiet room, free from distractions. (*"The monotony of a quiet life stimulates the creative mind"* - Albert Einstein, Physicist, 1877-1955). Work there at a clear desk. Initially develop a mind map (see Buzan, 1993), to help you select and arrange, into logical groups, the pertinent information solely from that which is in your mind.

With the resulting framework of the report decided, quickly compose the first draft **entirely from memory**, starting from the aims stated at the outset of the project. Do not stop if you cannot remember the details, just leave a gap. Your brain, i.e. your finest instrument, will automatically sift and sort the information to be presented into logical sequences. Never allow any complexities of the information to obscure the underlying scientific principles when writing. When composing this first draft, do not worry excessively about grammar, sentence structure, spelling or the exact choice of words. The logical flow of the text should not be inhibited by any associated uncertainties. The report can be thought of as a detective story, evolving from the clues to arrive at the conclusions, which should correspond exactly with the aims, as set out in the introductory section of the report. Collating (i.e. chunking) the available information under **succinct high-impact headings**, which are arranged subsequently in a logical sequence, tends to facilitate rapid understanding by the reader. It is usually far easier to "massage" - i.e. edit and polish, this first draft into the desired form, rather than to create it initially.

Once the first draft has been completed, introduce into it the detailed observations from your information diary and elsewhere. For instance, the basic assumptions made as well as a succinct up-to-date review of the relevant literature should be included, identifying any gaps in the available knowledge and what is likely to be new about the project. Relegate anything, e.g. supporting evidence, that disrupts the easy flow and continuity of thought, from the main body of the report to the appendices.

Self-editing your manuscript for clarity

Always think of your reader - it is preferable that your waste-paper basket is full (with earlier versions of the text) rather than your readers'! Rewrite anything that you suspect as being awkward or obscure, besides checking the grammar and spelling, while simultaneously trying to avoid wordiness and pomposity. Waffle and repetition in the report are wasteful. Your responsibility is to convey your information accurately and straightforwardly, rather than to try to impress your readers with knowledge, much of which may be slightly irrelevant to this particular report.

Avoid making unsubstantiated statements (i.e. assertions), without providing full references to their origins.

If feasible, set the second draft aside for a few days, and subsequently go through it critically, checking the grammar, punctuation and spelling. Use, for instance, "spell check" on your personal computer, as well as a thesaurus of synonyms and antonyms in order to improve the selection of appropriate words for your text and so, more exactly, communicate your intended meaning. Avoid the use of esoteric, undefined jargon. Then further criticize this draft - e.g. is it sufficiently succinct, logical and easily understood? Because you are very familiar with the topic you are writing about, you may presume too much with respect to your readers' knowledge and so your report can easily degenerate into being unintelligible to the average reader. On the other hand, it may be too verbose. Remember, even excellent writers have to edit out superfluous material. A good editorial maxim to implement is 'when in doubt (about the relevance or worthwhileness of a word, phrase or sentence), cut it out', i.e. elide such words and phrases as:-

"Obviously .... " (if it is truly obvious, why bother to say it?)
"It goes without saying that .... "
"It's hardly necessary to repeat that .... "
"I would like to start by saying that ...."
"Very" and "quite", which if used frequently lose effectiveness.

Similarly it is wise to shun the use of trite phrases known as clichés - see Appendix 7.2.

The editing process can be facilitated by printing out a hard copy, at least double-spaced, so that changes can then be inserted in red ink more easily. Sometimes, when a report is written by a team, this polishing of the document can be aided by displaying the typed sheets in a logical sequence simultaneously (e.g. around the walls of a room). This facilitates the revision of the manuscript, as well as the insertion of necessary information into the various sub-sections.

Some of the more pertinent questions and considerations regarding report writing are listed below:-

- Is the chosen title of the project a comprehensive yet brief (i.e. ≤ 12 words), accurate, eye-catching description of the content of the report? Will the key words in the title adequately facilitate other people locating your report via a computer search of the relevant literature?

- The title of your report (or of an article or a paragraph headline) should not have a full stop at the end of it. Most readers, to some extent unconsciously, tend to see such a stop as the end, and so are inhibited **slightly** from reading the rest of the message.

- Avoid the abstract and introductory sections exactly duplicating information in the title of the report.

- When you are checking what you have written, reading it aloud often enables you to spot errors and omissions that the eye alone would miss.

- Have you set out your "gems" as bullet points, rather than hiding them in a 'forest' of words?

- Have the **facts** been clearly differentiated from **opinions** throughout the report?

- Use questions, short paragraphs, clear attention-grabbing headings, readily-understood tables of data and well-labelled diagrams in order to capture your readers' interest.

- Is the information presented in the most logical and concise way?

- *"A drawing is worth a thousand words"* (Ancient Chinese Proverb.) Drawings and diagrams are usually easier to understand and eye-catching, especially if a data maximum or a minimum is exhibited - so make use of them to the best advantage.

- List your conclusions and recommendations, emphasising the more surprising ones.

- The three most common means of making references in the text to other relevant published literature (BSI, 1989; Bryar, 1994) are:-

    (i)   the "Running Notes" system;

    (ii)   the "Numeric or Vancouver" system; and

    (iii)   the "Surname and Date (or Harvard)" system.

The latter is used in this report: for this, the references are listed at the end of the report in alphabetical order, usually according to the surnames of the authors of the references. It is wise always, at least initially, to adopt this type of referencing. The introduction of further referenced material into the manuscript then avoids disrupting any number system for the references already in the text.

- Is sufficient information given so that each of the listed references can be traced easily?

- Concerning your supporting material, ask yourself whether it is:
    - relevant to your report?
    - accurate?
    - from a reliable source?
    - reasonably stated?
    - recent and topical?

- Have you desk-top publication facilities available? Ensure you get exactly the form of presentation you wish in order to increase its readability, e.g. with respect to font and print size, line spacings, margins and general lay-out, so as to obtain sufficient "white space" on each page?

- Are there any legal or security implications, should your report become publicly available? Have the required disclosure/confid-entiality agreements been obtained/satisfied?

- Be prepared to accept constructive criticism of your manuscript: this will help to improve the report before printing it, **with your name forever associated with it.**

APPENDIX 7.1   COMMENTS ON BIDDING FOR FINANCIAL SUPPORT FOR A PROPOSED RESEARCH PROJECT.

Before submitting an application, you should be able to satisfy the following:-

* From your review of the world's published literature, has a sufficiently interesting gap in knowledge, a conflict in previously-published conclusions or a need in society been identified?

* Is your new idea sufficiently original to justify receiving financial support on the scale envisaged?   Exactly what is the original contribution to knowledge, design, etc. that it is hoped will emerge from the project?   Indicate how you intend to add value to the requested investment.

* Are your aims sufficiently clear and worthwhile?

* Who are the likely sponsors - Research Councils, Charitable Trusts, EU, Industry, ...?   Which decision makers could possibly become the champions for your project?

The proposal should:-

* Indicate what is novel about the proposed project, and present documentation and statistics to support your assertions.

* Outline the likely benefits and relevance of the proposed project to your prospective sponsor. What outcomes could be exploitable?

* Provide a plan of attack for the project. This should include a detailed critical-path analysis and a bar chart describing the proposed time-schedule for the allocation of resources.   These indicate when progress/monitoring meetings with the sponsor will occur (e.g. every 3 months), and the likely imposed constraints on time and resource management.   Also, a detailed breakdown of costs (including overhead charges) should be supplied.

* Have attached to it, as an appendix, a copy of a typical legal contract used by your organisation when undertaking research for other bodies. It should indicate how confidentiality or publication of the

information revealed (as a result of completing the project) is to be ensured.

- Include a brief c.v. (see Chapter 4) for each of the proposed research-team members.

How can I **make my proposal sufficiently attractive** to a prospective sponsor?

- When selling, be positive with a clear message.

- During the present era of highly competitive quests for "research" funding, the more certain you are of the outcome of your proposed investigation, the greater the likelihood of receiving financial support for it. This state of affairs, unfortunately, tends to damn applications for the funding of pure research projects, whose conclusions almost invariably cannot be predicted beforehand.

- Lobbying the key people in the respective industry to gain their co-operation is often desirable prior to the formal meeting at which the decision, as to whether or not to approve the application, is to be made.

- If, as is likely, you are summoned to make an oral presentation concerning your bid, be (i) highly selective in your visual aids (e.g. OHP transparencies) so as to stress only the main points and (ii) enthusiastic.

About one month after the submission of your proposal, follow it up with a telephone enquiry concerning its progress. If you are not successful with your bid on this occasion, try to obtain some feedback or advice, so that you can improve future submissions. But never sound begging or desperate!

If all goes well, and you receive the requested funding, ensure that the legally-binding contract is acceptable to both parties, and duly signed. Records (including pertinent correspondence and financial accounts) should be maintained for at least five years after the completion of the contract: this period should be specified at the time the contract is signed.

APPENDIX 7.2 CLICHÉS (from the French for 'stereotype')

These words or everyday phrases have lost their freshness and become hackneyed. Often, clichés are a form of padding serving no useful purpose in a sentence. As Sir Ernest Gowers pithily wrote: *"Clichés are notorious enemies of the precise word"*. Some common clichés are:-

acid test
all of a sudden
all things considered
anything goes
as old as the hills
at the drop of a hat
at the end of the day
at this point/moment in time
bat an eyelid
blanket coverage
bored to death
(the) bottom line
catch-22 situation
conspicuous by his/her absence
dark horse
devour every word
don't count your chickens
eternal regret
explore every avenue
face the music
finger in every pie
fit as a fiddle
food for thought
for love or money
generous to a fault
green with envy
ground to a halt
happy accident
high and dry
horses for courses
I (we) hear what you're saying
inordinate amount of

in this day and age
it seemed an eternity
just not on
keep a low profile
keep your own counsel
make a killing
(the) mind boggles
name of the game
none the worse for wear
no peace for the wicked
no way
pinpoint accuracy
plain as the nose on your face
(if) push comes to shove
quick as a flash
resounding silence
rose between two thorns
search high and low
shot across the bows
skin of your teeth
stick to your guns
straight and narrow
suffer in silence
tender mercies
there, but for the grace of God,..
to all intents and purposes
tower of strength
up to his/her neck in debt
utter bilge
wash my hands of it
water under the bridge
with a vengeance

8 *PUBLIC SPEAKING: BEING A COMPELLING ADVOCATE*

"Whether we like it or not, power is with the person who can speak (effectively)" - *(Lord Salisbury, Prime Minister ,1830-1903).*

The Predicament

Three features matter concerning a speech:-

(i)   the reputation of the speaker
(ii)   his/her delivery of the message
(iii)   the content of the message

Of these, in rhetoric, the last is often the least influential. Therefore you should endeavour to speak with confidence, panache and enthusiasm, rather than, as often occurs, with timidity and nervousness. You can reveal a vast amount about your state of mind during an oral delivery - so beware! Do you bring in irrelevant detail and hesitate too often? Do you speak too quickly/slowly/harshly, at too high a pitch, with a sing-song or whining voice? Is your voice rasping, thin, harsh or monotonous? Do you sound boring or authoritative? Do you speak with such a strong regional accent or poor enunciation as to be almost unintelligible to the majority of your audience, and thereby reduce the positive impact of your words? Impeccable pronunciation is desirable as the standard English accent, but this is far from so with several regional dialects. Nevertheless do **not** try to hide your accent on an important occasion: the more you try, the less confident and convincing your voice sounds. A cultured Scots cadence can be equally, and sometimes even more, acceptable than the standard English accent, but this is far from so with several regional dialects.

Advice

• Having to give a formal talk can be a daunting task, even if the content is well prepared and the presentation properly rehearsed (Rawlins, 1993). You will probably be worried (see chapter 10) at the thought of having to speak in front of strangers, but you should regard this challenge as a self-educating opportunity.

• Self-consciousness is a major inhibitor in life: fear of failure is often the greatest single obstacle to achieving success. When we are excessively nervous, we become easily embarrassed and experience difficulty in 'thinking effectively on our feet', especially in trying to say exactly what we intended. The best recipe for reducing such nervousness is through thorough preparation: it leads to increased confidence and hence a better presentation.

• When speaking, practise the use of time-lock, i.e. eliminate from your thoughts worries with respect to the past, the future, or occurrences elsewhere; concentrate on doing well here and now.

• For a really important speech, each minute of the presentation may take an hour of preparation (i.e. researching, composing and editing the script). Then ask a respected colleague to criticise it, and re-write the offending/weak/inappropriate parts. Having a thoroughly-prepared script, including indications as to where to pause and give emphasis, will increase your confidence at the time of delivery, and hence the probability of the speech being a success.

• An accomplished speaker indicates by the tone of his/her voice which points in his/her speech should be emphasised.

Improved Human-Voice Delivery

Much can be done, by you, without having to resort to elocution lessons to improve the quality of your voice and the way you use it .

If you wish to become a highly-acclaimed public speaker, you need to breathe in and out more effectively, with greater inflation of your lungs. As we speak with more vigour when exhaling, we must manage our breathing carefully by relaxing the muscles responsible for inhalation and controlling the abdominal muscles needed for forced exhalation. Preferably, breathing should ensue from the centre of the human body i.e. below the rib cage, and not solely from the upper part of the chest, which should remain relaxed. By adopting such abdominal or diaphragm breathing, (i) your throat muscles will remain at ease; (ii) your voice tone and quality will improve, (iii) clearer speech will ensue, as well as (iv) higher sound intensities will be produced and so you will be able to project your voice further without strain.

You should master the easy abdominal-breathing exercise, which now follows:-

• **Lie on your back** with a substantial book supported by your stomach. Fully exhale, forcing air out of your body via your mouth. Then breathe in deeply through your nose, with your mouth shut. Repeating this exercise regularly, but slowly, helps develop the muscles involved in breathing. It also makes you more aware of the effective-breathing process. Try to increase the rise and fall of the book as you breathe in and then out successively.

• Adopt a relaxed, comfortable **standing position**, with your weight supported evenly by both balls of your feet. Then practise deep rhythmical, abdominal breathing: its frequency while speaking should be low, but influenced by the duration of the "sound bites", via which you express what you would wish to convey. The cycle of activities should normally be:-

    (i)   THINK - i.e. engage the brain

    (ii)   Take a DEEP ABDOMINAL BREATH silently but relatively quickly.

    (iii)   EXPRESS YOUR WORDS **SLOWLY** - while breathing out in a controlled manner.

    (iv)   PAUSE and THINK.

    (v)   Repeat the sequence from the beginning.

Be alert for poor enunciation, lack of clarity of your speech, incorrect pronunciation or slovenly articulation. Choose and say aloud a simple sentence, such as:-

        "Do you like green apples?"

or   "You said you love my sister".

Each time you repeat the sentence (when, for instance, you are driving and alone in your car or walking) put emphasis on a different word and introduce a pause in a different place in the sentence. See how the meaning changes!

To improve your pronunciation, repeat frequently:
  "Peter Piper picked a peck of pickled pepper. If Peter Piper picked a peck of pickled pepper, where's the peck of pickled pepper that Peter Piper picked.?"

Practise speaking more clearly and loudly than you do in everyday conversation (e.g.when you are alone), using sentences such as "Good morning, my name is Bond, James Bond". Determine the result of placing the emphasis differently, while varying your **pace** of delivery, pitch and loudness, and using pauses for effect, (the latter while breathing in) i.e. gain greater control. Keep your head held high while doing this and maintain steady eye-contact with your audience. Practise voice projection and correct articulation. Rehearse and improve what you say: recording and playing the tape back can be an embarrassing and challenging experience. Smiling, not grinning, occasionally, also tends to create empathy with your audience, but you may be unfortunate to be someone whose mouth naturally turns downwards at the corners, so even when relaxed, you appear to frown. Then it may be well worthwhile regularly exercising to gain more control over your facial muscles and to smile deliberately much more often.

You should aim to employ a well-modulated voice which sounds "warm" and sympathetic. A major mistake, which some lecturers make regularly, is to speak too softly. But more than loudness is required for achieving good voice-production. The four influential parameters are:-

(i)   **Pitch of your voice** - strive to lower it, in order to sound more impressive; a deep voice suggests that the speaker is confident.

(ii)   **Loudness** - which is dictated by the pressure of your outgoing breath, the physical fitness of your vocal chords, and the reinforcement ensuing as a result of the resonance achieved in the cavity formed by your nose, mouth and throat.

(iii)   **Speed of speaking** - Slowing this down will avoid imposing
        excessive stresses on your throat, make you sound more
        authoritative and give greater emphasis to what you are
        saying. Speaking rapidly leads to shallow breathing and
        heightened anxiety in the orator. A monotone delivery,
        mumbling or gabbling will lead rapidly to your losing your
        audience's attention.

(iv)   **Timbre of your voice tone** - as produced by your larynx -
        should be improved.

As a result of implementing these suggestions, you will sound gentler,
more controlled and assured. You will also tend to speak with greater
deliberation and so be more likely to be convincing.

A Public Lecture - Prior considerations

What is the purpose of the presentation - to inform, to teach, to sell, to
entertain,.....? Agree in detail what is required by the sponsor of the
conference/meeting concerning the proposed subject topic, the lecture
duration and the time constraints, well before the scheduled date of the
lecture.

*   Ascertain the **exact** location at which the lecture will be presented -
    see Appendix 8.1.

*   Determine the likely composition of the audience (with respect to
    age, gender, education level and socio-economic group) you will be
    addressing: target your lecture appropriately. For instance, does the
    intended audience consist of colleagues , clients, members of the
    press or a parent-teachers' association?

*   It would be helpful to know the likely number of people attending,
    e.g. so that an adequate number of handouts can be prepared.

*   It is wise if, before the lecture, you are able to identify a few
    members of the audience by their first names, so as to be able to
    draw them into the discussion during the course of the lecture. This
    stimulates even wider audience participation by entrainment of
    others.

- Practise, practise, practise........what you intend to present; try to be succinct but comprehensive.

Subject Matter

By developing a mind map (see Buzan 1993) on paper, collate the pertinent information into structural logical sequences. Acknowledge your sources of information. In order to increase its impact, try not to make more than three major clear-cut, interesting or even surprising conclusions (with corroboratory evidence) in your talk.

- Your speech needs a powerful, attention-grabbing introductory section, which outlines the main aim(s). Thus the purpose of the lecture should be stated clearly in its first few minutes. This is usually to **inform** (whereas that for a sales presentation is to **persuade**). The body of the lecture will present the supporting evidence.

- Avoid **boring** your audience (and hence wasting their time) by telling them only what is obvious or what they already know. Your audience (or readers) will be likely to ask "what's in it for me?", and cares little as to what you know, until they know how much you are concerned with their interests. So, target your presentations to exactly what your audience/sponsor/client/prospective employer really wants to find out or is valuable to them. Whatever you are offering should be needed.

- Prepare cue cards (see next section), which indicate the key words and pauses.

- Only use acronyms or acrostics if you are sure they will be readily understood.

- Do not waffle! Does each word of your presentation "pull its weight?"

- Finish the lecture on a bullish note. Ensure the climax is readily apparent to everyone. Your conclusions should re-affirm your main messages, but avoid introducing, at this stage, ideas or topics, which were not advocated earlier in your talk.

The Presentation

- When writing out your lecture/talk, plan where the pauses should occur and indicate these on your **cue cards**. These postcard-sized cards (tagged together, so that in the event of being dropped, they remain in the desired sequence): should contain only a few key points to remind you of what to say at that juncture in the lecture.

- Calm yourself in the half-hour immediately prior to the lecture by undertaking an appropriate relaxation mental exercise - see Chapter 10.

- In speaking persuasively you often have to be both an educator as well as an entertainer: therefore think of yourself as an "EDUTAINER".

- In making a public presentation, speak in a conversational style as though you are talking with a group of friends - your words will then tend to flow naturally and with humour - see also Appendix 8.2.

- No matter how many times you have practised or given this presentation previously, be enthusiastic during the lecture, and clearly focused in your comments.

- Wait for silence before starting. If you have not been introduced formally, outline your background, so indicating why you have been invited to give this lecture. Never say "I am not very good at this.....". Stand up straight, smile, and deliver with enthusiasm. Make it clear near the beginning, whether or not you would prefer to answer questions during or at the end of the lecture.

- You need to grab your audience's attention (e.g. with a startling statement or telling quotation from an eminent person) within the first 30 seconds. You should then state the aims of the lecture. Be brief and direct, using easily comprehensible language and avoid producing convoluted, sloppy or muddled sentences. The first four minutes of any meeting, usually leave a lasting impression. Therefore, you need to practise your opening words.

- Try to achieve eye contact with those with whom you are communicating, especially near the beginning and end of the presentation.

- Emanate a charming smile.

- Exhibit open body-language.

- A frequently-employed means of "hooking" your audience's attention is by asking a question, which, after a due pause, you then proceed to answer. Try pausing for longer than usual before answering an important question - silence tends to attract attention.

- Endeavour not to rush to deliver, which you will be inclined to do if excessively nervous. Don't speak quickly: it suggests/indicates to your audience that you are nervous. Relax your shoulders - your voice will then automatically be stronger. You will score more highly as a lecturer if you do not have other things on your mind when lecturing - i.e. practise **time-lock**. Because of the many conflicting requirements and associated stresses now imposed, for instance, upon middle managers, they tend frequently to give poor lectures.

- Remember, lecturing is a **performance** - it is never solely a verbal offering. You must exude confidence (which comes primarily through knowing your material well) and be positive. Despite having timed your presentation during several rehearsals, it is nevertheless wise to remove your wristwatch at the start of the lecture, and lay it, clearly in your view, on the lectern or the table on which your prompts are placed. When giving a lecture, to an unfamiliar audience, be conservative in your dress code - wear your darkest suit, a plain shirt and a visibly strong, but not distracting, tie (see Chapter 5)

- Throughout, deliver in an assured style:- an authoritative honest tone; poised presence; and be in control. Employ pauses between your statements, instead of what can be interpreted as negative, weakening words - viz, eliminate, 'but' 'however' and 'if' from your replies to questions.

- In the event of an external distraction, e.g. noise, what should you do? One famous engineering professor (Arthur Lefebvre), when his audience's attention was waning - a very rare occurrence for Arthur - used such a situation to his advantage. He opened the lecture-room door and called out *"Would you please stop making so much noise? - I have twenty students in here trying to get to sleep"*. Such an admonition besides stopping the noise generation outside, also re-invigorated his audience.

- Do not fiddle with your keys, loose change or tap your pen on the desk repeatedly – such nervous habits can be very distracting for your listeners.

- Note the reactions of your audience, e.g. when you see one or two of them yawning – beware, this can be contagious – invite the whole audience to stand up, and ask them to breathe deeply several times, relax their shoulders and subsequently clap their hands above their heads. This will increase the adrenalin flow and so enable them to concentrate better when they sit down again.

- Even the attentive members may easily forget the main points of your presentation. Therefore, it is wise to stress and repeat points, and present memorable examples during the lecture. If you really want to get your main messages and resulting desirable actions across, a single-sheet typed **hand-out** (well laid-out with plenty of 'white space' for the readers' annotations) should be issued. Ask a respected colleague to check the final draft of your hand-out in order to detect mistakes; frequently we see what we want/expect in our own scripts, rather than what is actually there.

- Video tape your performance while lecturing. Do you speak with your head slightly tilted to one side? Do you mumble? Do you rock from one foot to the other? All will be embarrassingly revealed!

Humour?

This can be helpful, but beware - it usually takes years of practice to develop the timing of a successful comedian. Thus use humour sparingly: the employed joke, quote or anecdote should enhance your basic message and so capture your audience's attention. However, jokes can easily misfire. To ensure your witticisms will be appreciated, the following suggestions are proffered:-

• Study your audience's reactions: if your humour is not appreciated, do not ignore the tell-tale signs (e.g. yawning, fidgeting or even snoring).

• Be politically correct in your use of words in order to avoid being accused of being sexist, racist, etc. For instance, when writing, 's/he' should be preferred to the personal pronoun 'he' if there is any possibility of the latter being interpreted as sexist.

• Only tease others/your audience gently and always avoid sensitive topics (such as overweight or baldness), especially when talking impromptu (see Appendix 8.3).

• Never ridicule anyone, or be sarcastic. Only a fool tries to make someone else look foolish.

• Be self-deprecating (but never a whinger). Surprisingly, this leaves a good impression. Others warm to you for not being pompous: it makes you more approachable.

• Avoid telling scabrous jokes.

What to Eliminate from your Utterances

We tend to use unnecessary repetitive words, especially when we are nervous. This can be annoying to the listener. Your response of "Really"? at the end of a statement, implies the speaker is lying. Preferably, the rejoinder should be "That's interesting" or "I didn't know that". Equally, the regular response of "yes" at the end of each statement is often perceived as disparaging rather than supportive.

- Avoid using the phrase "I presume" - it can sound patronising.

- Some speakers habitually say "I personally............", rather than just "I".This may be irritating. Avoid using "I sincerely......." too often: it implies that much of the rest of what you have to say is insincere.

- The habit of profanity and the use of slang are unacceptable in professional life and business: they are regarded as common, vulgar and unconvincing.

  "Mend your speech a little, lest you may mar your fortunes"
  - Shakespeare -King Lear (I, ii, 96-97)

- Have you eliminated from your utterances slovenly, audible pause-fillers? Examples of these are:-
  (i) redundant words, such as "ah", "er", "erh", "like", "O.K.", "right", "uh", "uhm", "um", "ya", "yea", "yeah" and "well";
  (ii) repetition of unnecessary phrases, for instance "ya' know", "I said" or "no way",
  and (iii) the habitual use of meaningless speech sounds, such as coughs, or irritating nervous giggles.
  These fillers emanate from us when our brains are not in complete control.

- The increasing use of grunts and Estuary English*, as well as declining grammatical standards are causes for concern. Ignoring the rules of a game inhibits one playing the game effectively. One's ultimate challenge should always be "Does confusion of thought lie behind, or result from, ugly expressions, careless pronunciation or poor use of words?" To be understood readily should be your main intention, rather than a desire for a pedantic adherence to the rules of grammar or spelling. A language preserved solely by an élite shrinks to jargon.

Footnote*   "Estuary English" was a phrase coined by David Rosewarne of Birkbeck College, London. He described it as a variety of modified regional speech in an article in The Times Educational Supplement of October 19th, 1984. Estuary English is in the continuum ranging from Received Pronunciation to London speech. Some interpret its spread as an expression of an increasingly classless society.

The Hostile Audience

• Try to anticipate, well in advance of the meeting, likely embarrassing objections or interruptions/demonstrations from members of the prospective audience. Anticipate what workable alternatives/options are available to your proposals. Rehearse your responses. Knowing you have well-prepared answers, ready for such challenges, increases your self-confidence.

• While lecturing, don't let your body language show that you sense you are facing hostility: adopt an open posture.

• Do not take the criticisms personally: stay calm and be polite.

• If a critical comment is forthcoming - STOP - even if you are in the middle of a sentence. It is usually wise to allow the questioner his/her full say.

• Encourage the dissenter to be constructive, e.g. to voice his/her feelings and opinions rationally. Thank the objector for raising these points. Convey a desire to co-operate to get to the heart of the matter. After all, many conflicts stem from misunderstandings.

• Identify anything positive, or that you can agree with in the objector's criticisms, i.e. summarize the main points of accord.

• Then discuss any other interesting points made by the objector.

• Explain (once again) but in an expanded form, what is your reasonable stance concerning the contentious issue. Try to deal with the negative aspects of the criticisms in an objective manner and summarize in your own words the points of disagreement. What is the relevance of the criticism? If you are mistaken, admit it.

• Discuss the benefits and disadvantages of all options in a calm, rational manner. Introduce facts and figures to support any assertions made. This may facilitate both you and the objector moving from one emotional commitment/entrenched position to a more logical objective reappraisal of the issue. Nevertheless, be prepared to agree to differ (and accept that subsequently, only someone senior to you may have the authority to decide on the solution to be adopted).

- Restate, in a restrained manner, the consensus conclusions. Remember, the original questioner will feel slighted or offended if these make him/her look foolish.

- Anger is a common, healthy emotion, which prepares you automatically, mentally and physically, to defend or attack. However, you should manage your anger, rather than let it control your behaviour. Anger needs an outlet (e.g. via physical exercise or by explaining **why** you feel angry with a respected colleague), otherwise it will evolve into destructive emotions such as rage, guilt, jealousy or hate, as well as lead to a serious deterioration of your health. There are many occasions (e.g., during a business meeting) where it is inappropriate to express your anger freely. When you have finished an emotionally-disturbing activity, try combining a relaxation technique with meditation - see chapter 10. Always remember that **your** anger arises from your perception of the situation, and, in this, you may not be one-hundred per cent correct!

- An essential skill is to avoid becoming angry or impatient as a result of having to answer penetrating questions, during or after a lecture, at an interview or during a viva-voce examination. Don't lose **your** temper under any circumstance - it is usually counter-productive. Remember, only **you** can allow **yourself** to lose your temper. By replying to a harsh, unjustified question in a modest, reasonable manner, with a positive premeditated concise answer, you will gain respect amongst the uncommitted members of the audience.

- If tempers in the audience run excessively high, call a break in the meeting, so that irrational opinions do not become too entrenched. Give yourself **at least** a half-hour break before responding to someone who has provoked you.

- Be diplomatic when a member of the audience states something which is incorrect: help rather than criticise.

- Don't resort to sarcasm with hecklers.

- It is alleged that one speaker when dealing with a persistently difficult heckler/questioner said: "I'd like to help you out - tell me, which way did you come in?" - Such a humorous quotation may defuse a difficult situation!

Eccentrics in your audience: how to deal with them

- With the **talk hog** (e.g. Harry), who tries to monopolise the questions session, you should interrupt eventually, **diplomatically**. (Remember, if you turn an enemy into a friend, you have eliminated an enemy). Lean forward on one foot, with your finger pointing to the ceiling, and say "Let me respond to that, Harry!". Answer the question, and immediately you finish, break eye contact with Harry and say "Let's hear from someone who hasn't spoken yet".

- With the **griper** (e.g. Charles), again exhibit diplomacy. Acknowledge the criticism with a comment to the effect that "I appreciate your concern and am glad that you brought it up. Does anyone else share this view?" Then, if appropriate, state: "Charles, as your complaint is so specialised, I suggest we deal with this later when more relevant facts are available."

- With the **heckler,** (e.g. Sophie) acknowledge what she has said and rephrase it for the rest of the audience. As the speaker, you can move towards Sophie: your close proximity may intimidate her. Alternatively invite her onto the stage to state her case. Frequently she will "bottle out" of this opportunity and thereby you have defused the situation. If not, ask "What is the relevance of your remark to the issue we are addressing?" In the face of incorrect accusations, hold your ground. Question the assertion(s) made. Keep challenging. Eventually, be conciliatory; offer to discuss the problem on a one-to-one basis at a mutually convenient time. By keeping calm throughout, you will emerge from the altercation with your reputation enhanced.

- With a known **subject matter expert** in the audience, recognise this expertise during the lecture and in any question session afterwards, but don't lose control of the occasion. However, try to harness any relevant knowledge that would be to the advantage of the audience.

- Strangely, the **quiet bored types** may present you with the biggest challenge. With them you will need frequent eye contact. Try to use their names to entice them into active participation. Ask questions that you know they can answer. Your lecture evaluation by the audience will then be more flattering.

- When dealing with **non-listeners**, state that what you are about to say is **confidential**, reduce the loudness of your voice and slow down your rate of delivery. The audience's attention will then be increased.

Handling a difficult or embarrassing question

- Listen carefully to the question: you may nod and/or smile to acknowledge your appreciation of the questioner's contribution during this period of conscious listening. Be patient.

- Eye contact is important in all oral communications, especially when responding to a difficult question. Make the initial eye contact with the questioner, but then look at others in the audience and return eye contact to the questioner just as you are about to finish your reply.

- Only use a prolonged gaze to **intimidate** someone. Usually, direct your gaze at the top of his/her head. Break your gaze downwards to the left or the right. Deliberate invasion of his/her space (i.e. by being in close proximity) is also disconcerting.

- An open-ended question (i.e. one to which a "yes" or a "no" answer is inappropriate) may tempt you into disclosing confidential or classified information, personal attitudes or apprehensions. Beware of (i) blurting out the first thought that comes to mind - it will probably not be the wisest rejoinder; and (ii) irrelevant verbose answers, which soon create a bad impression.

- Repeat the key concern of the questioner, in your own words, as the first part of your answer. Besides enabling you to clarify the question, it gives you time to marshal your thoughts.

- Develop the technique of invariably pausing (for up to a silent count of ten) to give yourself further time to organise your reply. Put your brain into gear before opening your mouth. Even if you have a well-thought-out reply, pause before answering. The audience will then tend to respect you more, for at least seemingly giving the question due thought. You will also be more likely to say exactly what you intended and so give a better response.

- If the questioner has deliberately chosen to misrepresent your point of view or put forward unwarranted criticisms, put the record straight.

- Answer succinctly the question asked or any part of it, if you can. Provide only the main item of persuasive in-depth information supporting your contention or assertion. You can however build into your answer, clues indicating that you have more corroboratory evidence available by saying "My primary/major example is ....."

- Discuss the background to the question, even if you cannot be unequivocal in your answer.

- Be candid. Never refuse to answer, e.g. by giving a "no comment" reply. This implies you have something to hide. However, don't bluff or fudge an answer. Admit it, if you don't know the answer "off-the-cuff". However, make a commitment that you will get back to the questioner with what information you have collated or can be disclosed, by a specified time (e.g. Friday of this week), provided s(he) leaves with you their fax or telephone number. Remember: no-one can know an exact, correct answer every time. If you are wrong, acknowledge it.

- Never end your answer with an excuse.

- Try to involve members of the audience in a general discussion of the question. There may be a **willing** expert present, but don't press-gang anyone, by name, without adequate warning into answering the question. Remember, deal with the members of your audience in exactly the manner you would wish to be treated yourself. For example, if you have no alternative but to redirect the question to an expert that you recognise in the audience, make certain s(he) has not been distracted (e.g. asleep) during the earlier proceedings. State his/her name, repeat the question, explain why s(he) is well qualified to respond and identify the name and the employing organisation of the **questioner**. This gives the expert, to whom you are "passing the buck", time to marshal his/her thoughts before having to speak.

• Following the discussion, ask the questioner, what his/her opinion is now on the matter, and be prepared to agree to disagree.

APPENDIX 8.1 VENUE AND FACILITIES

Attention Span

It is your reponsibility to ensure **your** audience remains comfortable and attentive throughout **your** lecture. Don't forget *"The mind will only absorb what the rear end is able to endure."* - **Mark Twain** *(1835-1910)*

Check list before giving the lecture.

*   Timing - Never leave your arrival so late that you have inadequate time to check the facilities before giving the lecture.

*   Equipment available? - Ensure that all the necessary demonstration models and equipment (e.g. blackboard with various coloured chalks, flip chart with coloured pens, OHP and slide projectors with screens, video recorder and appropriate display screen, microphone and speakers, opening windows and their blinds, and spotlight on the podium) are available.

*   Equipment working? - Is everything functioning properly? Are there enough electric-power sockets suitably located, together, if necessary, with adequate lengths of extension leads? Are you familiar with the eccentricities of the remote-controller, e.g. for the lights, humidity, blinds and projectors? Are the overhead-transparency and slide projectors suitably located and focused on the screen? Are the lenses of the projector clean, and spare bulbs and fuses available?

*   Will the audience see clearly? - Ensure any projected images are not distorted (e.g. if necessary, adjust the screen to be out of the vertical plane). Is there anything (e.g. an alternative projector) suspended from the ceiling that interrupts the projection beam? Can the room be adequately blacked out? Ensure that your transparencies and slides are in the right sequence, and that their images will appear as required during the lecture (i.e. not inverted or laterally reversed) on the screen. If possible, use a foot switch for controlling the projector, so leaving both your hands free to remove and substitute transparencies on an overhead projector.

- Will the audience hear clearly? - Well prior to the lecture, with only a technician and yourself present, practise projecting your voice to the most remote seat in the auditorium. Adjust the sound levels for the microphones and video players appropriately: remember, an audience absorbs sound, and so in the "empty" auditorium, be over-generous with the loudness setting.

- Will the audience be comfortable? - Are the seats arranged as required? Will the room maintain a comfortable temperature when full of people?

- Will you be comfortable? - Will there be a glass of fresh water available for you on the lectern during the lecture?

Such attention to detail shows your respect for the interests of your audience - this investment will create a positive impression.

Start and finish the presentaiton with the room lights fully on, so that then, at least, you can achieve eye contact with members of the audience.

Visual Aids

The use of visual aids facilitates the effective communication of complicated ideas (see Pike, 1989). "Showing" and "telling" simultaneously increases the audience's attention and retention.
Confucius said " A picture can be worth a thousand words". Using projected images reduces the mental stress on you as the lecturer by diverting intermittently your audience's gaze to the screen (or demonstration). Alternatively, as an inexperienced lecturer you can use the image on the screen as a prompt to what you wish to say next. But the more you become proficient as a lecturer, the less necessary you will find the use of visual props (e.g. OHP transparencies, slides and flip charts). The following advice may prove to be helpful:-

- Know your visual aids so well that you do not have to worry about them during your presentation, i.e. rehearse, rehearse, rehearse,........

- Don't read out the words on the screen: let **your** audience read them. Give the audience about 50% more time to scan the text on the screen than it takes for you to read it - they will take longer because it is new to them.

- Only switch on the projector immediately prior to when you need the image of the next transparency. Switch off the OHP before changing transparencies. Never remove a transparency from the projector while the OHP is still on: the resulting glare is painful and disrupting for you as the lecturer.

- Don't leave the projector switched on when you have finished dealing with the content of the image of a particular projected transparency or slide.

- Stand to the right (as viewed from the audience) of the screen when lecturing. As images on the screen will tend to be read from left to right, the audience's gaze will then continually be drawn back to you.

- Don't turn your back to **your** audience in order to operate the projector (or to use a flip chart).

- Never stand between the screen and **your** audience.

- If you use a telescopic (e.g. a car's recycled radio-aerial) or laser pointer to draw attention to key points on the screen, do so while facing the audience.

- Have a spare bulb available for the projector.

Visibility of the information presented

KILL - keep it large and legible!

Will the words or symbols be clearly legible to the most-distant viewer in the lecture theatre? The Deardon standard provides guidance for this and suggests, as a reasonable recommendation, that the **minimum** height H (in cm) of the projected image of an individual letter of the alphabet on the screen should equal 10 A/X, where A is the presentation area (in m^2) of the whole screen and X is the distance (in m) from the screen to the furthest viewer. For example, if the area of the screen is 13.5m^2 and the longest distance from the screen to the most remote back seat is 15m, then each letter on the screen needs to be at least 9cm in height.

Slides

* These tend to be much more expensive than transparencies, and so more consideration will be given in this text to the latter, though some of the remarks made here will be applicable to the former.

* For 35mm slides, a light-coloured text against a dark background is relatively easy to read. (For OHP transparencies, the reverse tends to be true.)

* Number each of your slides to help you to know that they are in the desired **sequence** and not **inverted.**

* Use black/dark blue slides for intermissions between topics.

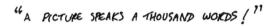

OHP Transparencies

- Each of these should be designed to create a high impact: for instance, any text presented should be succinct (i.e. clear and concise) and not cluttered with confusing detail.

- Underline the title, which should be understood readily.

- Include only one theme/concept per transparency in order to avoid appearing jumbled.

- Per transparency:- ≤ 5 words per line, ≤ 5 lines, ≤ 3 colours: otherwise the message becomes obfuscated. Avoid using orange or green, which are not particularly distinctive when projected.

- After each bullet point, employ a few concise words: this should be easier to comprehend rather than a whole sentence.

- Large thick script conveys confidence: small thin letters create an impression that the lecturer is diffident.

- Hand-written transparencies tend to look untidy and amateurish.

- Use a transparent cover – commercially available (e.g. from 3M) – for each transparency. You can then write on the cover during the presentation of that transparency, without damaging it.

- Use a mix of capital and lower case letters.

- Sans Serif fonts, such as HELVETICA, tend to be easier to read than Gothic script or letters.

- Use a bar or pie chart to indicate relative magnitudes. It is a common convention, with a pie chart, to locate the largest slice in the upper right-hand quadrant, and thereafter the slices are arranged in order of decreasing magnitude in the clockwise direction.

- A graph, especially if it exhibits a maximum or minimum, is usually much more persuasive than a table of values. The lines indicating the trends should appear thicker than the axes, without any other confusing lines appearing on the figure. If more than one parameter's variation is shown, use colours and/or dashed or dotted lines to achieve greater clarity. All labels should be displayed parallel to the abscissa axis.

- As a rough guide to the legibility of the image of an OHP transparency on the screen, you should be able to read the **transparency** easily when it is held vertically 2 metres in front of you.

- In order to restrict attention to only one part of the transparency, use an opaque piece of paper, which can be moved appropriately to hide the feature(s) not under discussion.

- To indicate a specific feature, lay a pointer on the overhead transparency, which is being projected.

Flip charts

Several of the comments made regarding transparencies also apply to flip charts. (See Brant, 1986).

- Before the start of the lecture, ensure that the lower part of each sheet is easily separated from its neighbour. Then you will be able, during the lecture, to flip the sheets over readily without any danger of pulling the tripod support on top of you - this has been known to happen to nervous lecturers.

- It is preferable to use green marker pens (especially in poor lighting conditions) except for making points which you would wish particularly to emphasise - these should appear in red. Avoid using blue.

- It is wise to prepare most of each of your charts well in advance of the lecture. This will avoid you devoting an excessive amount of time during the lecture writing out obvious points or making a pertinent schematic drawing while addressing your audience.

However, leave plenty of gaps on each flip chart for additional facts and figures to be added (in black) during the presentation.

- On such previously-prepared flip charts, when necessary, lightly **pencil in** reminders, notes or pre-drawn diagrams. These will be so faint as not to be visible to the seated audience, but could be of enormous help to you, for instance in drawing a circle.

- Subsequently, on some occasions, it may be beneficial to display the completed flip charts, in logical sequence, around the walls of the lecture room. This can be accomplished with the aid of masking tape or "Blu-Tack", without damaging the decoration of the room.

Video

- When relevant material is so viewed, the topic can be brought to life within the confines of the lecture room.

- Ensure the video recorder and T.V. are functioning properly. This should be checked by previewing the video tape to be used - always a desirable practice.

- For greatest effect, and **after** having discussed a topic, the lecturer should run the video (preferably for a maximum of 8 minutes at one time) to substantiate the points made. The process should then be repeated, i.e. the lecturer's delivery followed by the video support. This sequenced approach will facilitate the audience's understanding of the concepts presented.

- As the lecturer, you should stay in the room while the video is being viewed.

APPENDIX 8.2   ACHIEVING EFFECTIVE CONVERSATIONS

• Treat each person you meet as being important, and give them your full attention.

• Always be polite, considerate and diplomatic with the person with whom you are speaking, irrespective of their seniority.

• Listen attentively without interrupting the speaker.

• Avoid making destructive criticisms, indulging in gossip or propagating rumours. If you do gossip, only talk about the attributes of others, never their weaknesses or faults.

• Use praise rather than sarcasm or ridicule.

• Never patronise or put colleagues 'on the spot'.

• Drop pretension - speak to be understood.

• If you have nothing to say, keep quiet. You will then command much more attention when you speak.

APPENDIX 8.3   SPEAKING IMPROMPTU

Generally, it is wise to assume you will be asked to 'say a few words' on many occasions to which you are invited. Therefore, have pertinent thoughts, well prepared, in your mind. Then you will amaze the others present with your "impromptu" skills.

When asked "unexpectedly" to speak at a formal or unofficial meeting (e.g. a wedding reception):-

(i)   Stand up and "walk-tall", slowly and deliberately in order to face your whole audience.

(ii)   Never allow yourself to be hurried.

(iii)   Adopt a proprietorial manner, rather than a furtive attitude as though you did not belong there.

(iv)   Pause to permit time to assemble your thoughts.

(v)   Do not excessively express your gratitude for the opportunity to speak.

(vi)   State your points loudly and clearly, with pauses between to achieve emphases.

(vii)   Add one supporting example or relevant anecdote with each of your three (or less), main statements.

(viii) Resist the temptation to say "thank you" at the end of your remarks.

9   *PERSUASIVE POWERFUL PRESENTATIONS*

To be forceful, you need to think like a psychologist and use a compelling vocabulary (see Appendix 9.1). Your audience, whether visible or not (e.g. see Appendix 9.2) must want to agree with you. Thus:-

- Be a purveyor of hope.

- Be enthusiastic. *"If you are not fired by enthusiasm, you may be fired with enthusiasm."*

- Where possible press the flesh, e.g. use touch via a handshake. The response you receive then tends to be more positive.

- Don't make subjective judgements. Avoid the use of nebulous/non-concrete sentences containing words such as "best". Instead, employ statements you can prove - e.g. he is the fastest or she is fluent in Spanish, rather than s(he) is the best.

- Don't make assertions which cannot be substantiated. Opinions have no place in logical objective analyses or arguments.

- Be fair, firm and honest about all of the options you and your colleagues are considering together. If the others realise that you are unbiased, increased faith in you will ensue.

- Don't drive others into "mental" corners, from which they can extricate themselves only by losing face. (Remember that you can modify behaviour, but it is almost impossible to alter attitudes.)

- Never lose your temper at a committee meeting, with an external examiner or during an interview.

- Don't be dismissive about other people or their suggestions.

- Above all, show more interest in your audience than in yourself, but be open about yourself if pertinent questions are asked. Be friendly and not pompous, but steer clear of being over-familiar.

- Endeavour to make those around you smile or even laugh.

Presentations: Content & Delivery

Your presentation should:-

- be relevant to your audience's needs and pitched at their level of understanding.

- state your clear objectives, preferably as a series of bullet points, early in the introductory section.

- be detailed but succinct, i.e. concise as a result of being well targeted, i.e. KISS - keep it short and specific.

- have a single-core theme running throughout.

- only include assumptions which are reasonable.

- have a readily-apparent logical structure.

- exhibit primacy and recency.

- employ well-understood language, e.g. avoid jargon.

- have each major point of your argument reinforced by an illustrative example or supporting evidence.

- avoid (i) burying the essential message by confusing or irrelevant detail – i.e. information pollution, or (ii) likely-to-be misleading statements, which can so easily create embarrassing ambiguities.

- be delivered in a relaxed, confident manner.

- avoid employing the "hard sell", but show your skills at marketing ideas and opinions. Fewer people would order a steak if it were described (quite accurately) as an "old chunk of dead cow".

APPENDIX 9.1 - SELECTED POWERFUL WORDS
These can be employed in attention-grabbing headlines:-

Now	Today	Immediately	Powerful
Dynamic	Protect	Proven	Create
Results	Trust	Free	Bonus
Money	Profit	Save	Safe
Discover	Learn	Understand	Known
Help	Love	Health	You

APPENDIX 9.2 IMPROVING YOUR TELEPHONE TECHNIQUE

Most people tend to (i) waffle and/or (ii) be ineffective listeners when using the telephone, so that such conversations are far too long and expensive. However, these bad habits can be overcome by implementing the following:-

- **Prepare** (preferably on paper) in advance, as a series of bullet point notes, exactly what you wish to say. What information do you need to convey or obtain? What questions would you like answered?

- Don't say "Hello" when answering the 'phone: preferably use a greeting and then give your name and that of your department.

- Ensure you know who you are speaking to, and what his/her position is. Jot down immediately the phonetic spelling of his/her name. This can save subsequent embarrassment.

- Try to develop a more positive telephone manner. Are you sufficiently enthusiastic when phoning?

- Employ **time-lock**. Also concentrate by shutting out all local distractions (to the telephone conversation) such as by closing your eyes.

- In general, **don't interrupt** the person at the other end of the telephone line. A pause is acceptable: it indicates that you are thinking about what s(he) has said.

- Note down immediately any important points that arise during the conversation.

- **Ask direct questions** concerning any existing ambiguities or the needs of the person telephoning.

- **Don't make premature assumptions, precipitous conclusions** or hasty decisions. If necessary, say you will ring back when the affected people have been consulted, and then do so!

- Try to **visualize the person** with whom you are speaking.

- Replying occasionally with *"I see"* or *"I understand"* shows your interest.

- Improve the effectiveness of your use of the telephone by smiling when you speak on it.

- When dealing with irate callers, be calm and helpful! Ascertain the exact cause of their complaint or problem. If you are unable to deal with it yourself there and then, ask for their name and phone number, and arrange for the appropriate person to address it as soon as feasible.(see also Chapter 8, Appendix 8.3)

- Sometimes however, a telephone caller can 'corner you' such that you are inadequately prepared to deal with his/her request. Then use a ploy to "free up time" for you to think carefully, e.g. say "I am in a meeting" or "I am not at my desk", "May I call you back at 5.30p.m?" If the telephone conversation persists and becomes difficult, but you do not wish to commit yourself any further, break the connection while **you** are still speaking, or knock on your desk and shout "Come in".

- When recording a message for your answering machine, state your name and speak slowly and clearly: give exact instructions about recording the message, and ask for a telephone number so that you can ring back. However, try to avoid the hassle of having to deal with some of the enquiries that would otherwise accumulate on your answer-phone. Reply, by providing at the end of your recorded message a further telephone number, via which you can be contacted in the event of an emergency.

10   ANXIETY MANAGEMENT

"If you are distressed by anything external, the pain is not due to the thing itself, but to your estimate of it. Thus you have the power to revoke it at any minute". - Marcus Aurelius, Roman Emperor and Philosopher (121-180 A.D.)

The Problem

We all tend to be apprehensive before a public-speaking engagement or an interview, sometimes even though we are well prepared and well qualified with respect to the content of what we wish to say. In the extreme case, when subjected to this high mental-stress, panic sets in and our mind goes blank.

The common **tell-tale symptoms** of excessive mental-stress, anxiety and/or nervousness in a lecturer/interviewee are often combinations of:-

* increased frequency of eye-lid blinking

* biting or licking of lips

* frequent throat-clearing and/or hair preening.

* finger tapping, quick uncoordinated gestures or hands in pockets.

* when standing, rocking from side-to-side or twisting your feet so that their sides bear all your weight.

The Solution.

Irrespective of how you feel, to be successful, in a highly-stressful situation, try to avoid emitting such negative signals to your audience/interview panel. Appear to be completely in control! This will lead to a positive feedback from those around you, e.g. with respect to the confidence they accord you, and hence raise your latent self-esteem at this critical time. How this can be achieved is revealed in the following:-

- **Worry** is negative goal-setting: it usually involves imagining (and talking) about exactly what you do **not** wish to happen. The more one is worried, usually the poorer are our powers of judgement at that juncture:then it becomes difficult to struggle out of the "trough of despair". The antidote is to engage in purposeful actions to eliminate the cause of the worry and engage in time-lock.

- You are motivated to act positively by realising the benefits of what you will thereby accomplish. This will boost your self-image. Behave as a brave man, even if you are terrified!

- We need **will-power**: this positive skill can be developed, strengthened with practice and directed to help us achieve our targets. Devise specific quantitative objectives. Divide these into a series of small goals. Anticipate stumbling blocks and plan how to overcome each of them.

- It is wise to impose upon yourself such a sequence of small quantitative objectives, which have to be reached within specified periods. This time-management procedure usually involves having a main long-term target. If you make a habit of adhering to rolling-plan priority lists, worked out as daily schedules, you will gain the confidence to confront ever new challenges. This will develop your will-power.

- It is important to realise that when you are **relaxed,** it is easier to work or learn effectively. Enjoyable events tend to be remembered more clearly! Therefore, you should strive to produce a low-stress, friendly environment in order to be highly creative and hence achieve greater productivity.

- Eliminate irritants from your life, e.g. especially on important occasions, avoid wearing tight clothing which makes you squirm.

The cumulative beneficial effect of implementing these suggestions is often surprising.

Practical procedures for reducing inter-related physical and mental tensions.

- When appropriate opportunities arise, relax physically. One recommended routine is:-

  Loosen your clothing and take off your shoes (e.g. when flying). Sit comfortably, but upright, with both feet on the floor, your hands in your lap and eyes closed.

  Tense/tighten one major muscle-group in your body (for ~10 seconds) and then relax, i.e. become limp. This should be carried out for each of the muscle groups in turn:-
  - (i)   toes and feet
  - (ii)   legs
  - (iii)   stomach
  - (iv)   arms and hands
  - (v)   shoulders and neck
  - (vi)   head and in particular the face.

  Then stand up, stretch each of your legs individually with toes pointed, buttocks squeezed together and arms held upright. Relax. The whole sequence should be repeated several times.

- In a quiet environment, when you are alone, practise deep abdominal breathing for about 20 minutes each day. Unhurriedly inhale through your **nose**, and subsequently exhale through your mouth, allowing your whole body to become relaxed - from your toes to the top of your head. Repeat this procedure. Do not pause between inhalation and exhalation of breath. As you breathe out, repeat a meditation mantra (e.g. "caring") silently to yourself, or imagine walking along your favourite quiet beach, in warm sunshine, with a slight breeze on your back. For those suffering from a high level of imposed mental stress, practising regularly, each day over an extended period (~3 months), such a meditation/relaxation technique, can dampen the perceived pain of many situations as well as be enlivening.

- Practise your normal activities, while breathing deeply and easily with your muscles relaxed. When required, only bring into play that part of the muscle system which is necessary. By automatically relaxing your muscles outside these enforced-activity periods, you will have far more controllable effort available when you really need it.

- Get into the habit for ~10 minutes per day of practising **passive concentration**, i.e., focusing your thoughts on what is happening without trying to attain any particular goal. You may achieve this by taking a hot bath: it is amazing how solutions to problems will then emerge unexpectedly, or lines of profitable endeavour will suggest themselves, to your already prepared mind.

- Taking regular physical exercise and becoming fit, e.g. three 20-minute sessions in the gymnasium or playing badminton each week will, within 3 months, make you far less anxiety-prone. Even gardening regularly will facilitate this.

- These techniques can help you relax. Many people turn **excessively** to drinking alcohol or watching T.V. for this purpose: on some occasions, however, these can "psyche you up" and so have the opposite effect, i.e. make you even less capable of coping with reality.

11   PRESCRIPTION FOR SUCCESS

"He is a wise man who does not grieve for the things which he has not, but rejoices for those which he has" - **Epictetus, Greek Philosopher (c.60 -110AD)**

The essential elements for a successful presentation are pertinent knowledge (e.g. through comprehensive preparation), enthusiasm, but above all CONFIDENCE. You need a positive mental attitude, i.e. you should motivate yourself to believe that you are successful. Thus, the rest of this chapter provides basic advice to help you increase your confidence, and hence achieve success in communicating your thoughts commensurate with your intelligence and experience.

Success is a state of mind and not an absolute condition: it is often a matter of perception. For example, someone earning £100,000 p.a. may feel a failure, whereas another earning £10,000 p.a. believes s(he) is successful. Unfortunately, too often in the 1990s, gaining a financial profit is regarded as the main criterion of success.

The older we get, the more good reasons we know for avoiding taking risks. As children, we have high self-esteem and willingness to take risks, but as we grow up, the 'slings and arrows of outrageous fortune', assail us and often lead to excessive anxiety and undermine our innate confidence. We become increasingly conscious of our vulnerability. However, this adverse trend can be reversed by :

    (i) the cumulative effect of regular small successes,
    (ii) having several of "irons in the fire", and
    (iii) believing you will get there in the end.

It should also be remembered that an occasional rebuff can lead to a more objective perspective; a modicum of humility displayed in our relationships with others is an essential ingredient in being continually successful.

Characteristics of Successful People

There is no unique recipe for achieving sustainable success. Nevertheless, there are many attributes regularly exhibited by winners, who generally are:-

- clear sighted about their usually self-imposed target(s) for achieving improvement(s).

- flexible in their approaches to accomplishing objectives.

- willing to "lose a battle in order to win the war".

- appreciative of constructive feedback.

- fully committed to finishing tasks.

- focused on **accomplishments**, i.e. outcomes, rather than on the associated **activities**: it is usually more rewarding to satisfy a few challenges well, rather than undertake many more in a superficial fashion

- willing to learn.

- well-organised and effective planners.

- able to recognise opportunities, which are seized eagerly.

- independent thinkers.

- punctual, with a strong sense of urgency.

- swift, vigorous implementers of decisions, without either prevarication or procrastination.

- ambitious, determined and performance orientated.

- competitive and persistent, with a hunger to win.

- reliable as well as talented.

- able to produce their best efforts when it matters most: in other words, "when the going gets tough, the tough get going".

- habitual TIME-LOCK implementers, who concentrate on the task in hand and make every day "count".

- relaxed and patient, whatever the circumstances.

- comfortable with their seniors, or have learned to appear so.

- modest when speaking of their status, accomplishments and family: with respect to university degrees - "get them and forget them". In general conversation, e.g. when phoning, it is advisable to avoid using your title. *"I know of no case when a man added to his dignity by standing on it"* - **Winston S. Churchill (1874-1965).** Self-praise is a drug on the market, whereas self-mockery has a charm and selling power all of its own.

- courteous and obey the rules of etiquette.

- discreet and never gossip.

- loyal to their colleagues and friends.

- purveyors of hope, making sure that 'the light at the end of the tunnel' is never switched off.

Steps to success

There is no unique formula for achieving success, but the following advice and opinions should prove helpful.

- By craving or searching for happiness, you will never find it.

- Not getting what you want is often regarded, in retrospect, as a stroke of luck.

- We learn wisdom from failure much more than from success. We often discover what will do, by finding out what will not do. *"Probably he, who never made a mistake, never made a discovery"*. - **Samuel Smiles, Scottish Author (1812-1904).**

- Concentrate on the reasons for a failure, rather than on attributing the blame for it.

- To be consistently successful, decide what major goal is worth pursuing. Know exactly what the target looks like before trying to hit it. But be flexible as to your tactics for achieving the goal.

- Analyse, before setting out, with the aid of a pertinent "map", what lies ahead on your journey. Make full use, in advance, of what relevant information you have available - this will result in a reduction of the expended effort. Preparation always pays dividends!

- Those who fail to plan are unconsciously planning to fail.

- Be well-organised: the more effectively you plan and prepare your work, the more often you will be lucky.

- *"The time to repair the roof is when the Sun is shining".* - **J.F. Kennedy, USA President (1917-1963)** In other words, do things before they need to be done - this increases the likelihood of you being a winner.

- Always expect the unexpected.

- Treat problems as opportunities for growth and increased self-mastery.

- Providence consists largely of what you make of what happens. It is not the problem, but how we deal with the problem that dictates whether or not we are successful.

- Act with initiative and courage, as if the whole enterprise depends on you.

- Be thrifty in the use of time. Wherever you are, always have some work with you that you can tackle while waiting (e.g. for a plane).

- Know when you work most effectively (e.g. during the morning or late at night; when relaxed or under stress) and so schedule and prioritise accordingly.

- Chance favours the prepared mind, i.e. you need to acquire the pertinent skills.

- Maintain a positive mental attitude irrespective of the circumstances.

- *"Whether you think you can or think you can't - you are right."* - **Henry Ford, Car manufacturer (1863-1947).** What usually matters is not what you can't do, but rather what you can and will do.

- Be both physically and mentally fit. *"True enjoyment comes from activity of the mind and exercise of the body: the two are ever united."* - **Baron Alexander von Humboldt, German naturalist and statesman (1769-1859).**

- The majority of illnesses are psychosomatic: therefore always try to be positive and cheerful.

- Eliminate guilt: don't fiddle your expenses, taxes or benefits - and don't cheat on colleagues.

- Carry very little mental "luggage": avoid clutter of the mind, i.e. information pollution.

- Devote **your** full attention to the person(s) with whom you are now **conversing**: do not permit your concentration at this time to be disrupted by pre-occupations with, for instance, your over-due tax return or the health of a member of your family. Practise time-lock: too often, today is the tomorrow you worried about yesterday.

- Where feasible, tackle you problems one-by-one: put your concentrated energy into satisfying a single task at a time.

- Praise, encourage, support, compliment, smile........they cost nothing but give a lot.

- People like to associate with those who enjoy life and are successful.

- During a crisis, it is beneficial to have such friends/allies, who are prepared to help.

- Success rarely comes to grumblers: you are paid to think, not to whine; never look upon the past with regret.

- Never bring a problem to your boss, without at least one proposed solution.

- If you are relaxed, despite the imposed mental stresses, you tend to succeed.

- If you over-extend yourself, you wreck your chances of success. However, avoid being so comfortable that a mediocre performance ensues. Thus, we need optimal settings for our mental and physical aspirations.

- Encourage those around you to believe in themselves. This basic skill of a good teacher builds confidence in your team.

- Have faith in yourself based upon your track record.

- A new idea or a desired sequence of words is sometimes lost, unless noted immediately.

- If you don't object to unwelcome changes that you believe are wrong, they may be implemented by default, with others thinking you approve of them.

- Be determined - never waver.

- Sacrifice and persistence, in order to overcome negative thinking and dissipative activities, will lead to success eventually.

- Commitment and integrity are essential for achieving long-term success.

- *"Things may come to those who wait, but only those things left by those who hustle"*. - **Abraham Lincoln, U.S. President (1809-1865).**

- To lower the mental stress upon yourself, try to be the decision-maker.

- Try to set the agenda for your actions: you will then tend to set the pace, last the course and so win more often.

- When you rush, you increase the probability of making mistakes. Therefore, be calm and patient, but with a sense of urgency.

- Beware of confiding in anyone: few are able to keep a secret.

- Always have an answer to the question - "What would I do if I were sacked tomorrow?"

- *"The only thing we have to fear is fear itself"*. **Franklin Delano Roosevelt, U.S. President (1882-1945)** Fear often arises because of ignorance. What you fear can often be overcome by taking appropriate action. Postponing such an action usually only leads to the intensity of the fear increasing.

- If you are afraid of something, you are giving it power to control you.

- You gain strength, courage and confidence by every experience in which you have to look fear in the face.

- Keep cool in the face of turmoil: don't make a drama out of a crisis.

- By emulating the behaviour of someone you respect, you will then tend to exhibit the traits that you admire in him/her.

- What happens is usually not as significant as how you react to the circumstances. Be resilient when faced with a negative situation!

- Win without boasting .... and lose without excuses.

- Take account of your instincts, as well as the facts.

- Behave in the same way unto others, irrespective of whether you have been successful or failed. Treat **everyone** in the organisation with respect and dignity.

- Loyalty begets loyalty, trust begets trust, friendship begets friendship and commitment begets commitment.

- Always finish stronger than when you started.

- Many of life's failures are people who did not realise how close they were to success when they gave up.

How to Change your Behaviour or your Situation.

(i)   What do you want (e.g. a tidy office)? What is preventing you from achieving it?

(ii)   Why is this change an improvement? How would it improve your efficiency? Why is it urgent to start to do it now?

(iii) Keep a note pad and functioning pen with you at all times (e.g. beside your bed, in the bathroom, in you car, etc) to jot down pertinent ideas as they arise.

(iv)   Set a time schedule for achieving the complete change. Get a respected friend to check on your progress.

(v)   Compare your new lifestyle with your former one.

(vi)   Beware of the complacency of success - don't let your new standards decline.

(vii) Remember, work smarter, not just harder.

Valedictory Advice

Your worst enemy is often yourself. *"The only battles you lose in advance are the battles you don't fight"* - **Jacques Chirac, President of the French Republic (1932 -)**

REFERENCES AND BIBLIOGRAPHY

R.C. BRANT — Flip charts: How to draw them and how to use them. Pfeiffer & Company, San Diego, CA, 1986.

R. BRYAR — The world of referencing: Nursing Times, Vol 90. No.36, pp. 38-41, 1994.

W.BRYSON — Mother tongue: - the English language, Hamish Hamilton, London, 1990.

BSI — Recommendations for references to published materials: BS 1629,British Standards Institution, London, 1989.

T. BUZAN — The mind map book - radiant thinking. BBC Books, London, 1993.

D. COHEN — How to suceed in psychometric tests, Sheldon Press, London, 1993.

W. DAVIS — Best of success: C.E. Publishing Co. Lombard, Illinois, U.S.A. - 15th printing, 1992.

B. LAMB — National survey of communication skills of young entrants to Industry and Commerce. Biology Department, Imperial College, London SW7 2BB, 1994. (Price £3.50)

B.DECKER — You've got to be believed to be heard: St Martin's Press, New York, 1992.

L. MAUNDER and S.D. PROBERT (Editors) — Experimentation for students of engineering: Vol. 1, Heinemann Educational Books, London, 1972.

T. McARTHUR (Editor)   The Oxford companion to the English
                       language: Oxford University Press, 1992.

D. PEOPLES   Presentations plus: proven techniques: John
                       Wiley & Sons, NewYork:, 1988.

C.PIKE   Visual aids in business: A guide to effective
                       presentations, Crisp Publications Inc, Los
                       Altos, CA,1989.

K. RAWLINS   Presentation and communication skills: a
                       handbook for practitioners. Macmillan Ltd,
                       London, 1993.

P. ROBERTS   Plain English: Penguin Books Ltd,
                       Harmondsworth, UK, 1987

D. SARNOFF   Never be nervous again: Crown Books, New
                       York, 1994.

N. STIMSON   How to write and prepare training materials:
                       CA Pfeiffer & Company, San Diego, CA,
                       1991.

L. STONEALL   How to write training materials: Pfeiffer &
                       Company, San Diego, CA, 1991.

A.WELLS   Get back to basic skills: The Sunday Times,
                       London, 6:18, 16th October 1994.

L.YOUNG   The naked face: Arrow, London, 1994.

INDEX